Blessing my mother's rosary

I shall be telling this with a sigh
Somewhere ages and ages hence:
Two roads diverged in a wood, and I—
I took the one less traveled by,
And that has made all the difference.

Robert Frost, *The Road Not Taken*

Blessing my mother's rosary

Lourdes.
Loss.
Love.

CARLA KNOROWSKI

Blessing My Mother's Rosary
Lourdes. Loss. Love.
by Carla Knorowski

Cover design by Nancy Horvat
Interior design and typesetting by Andrea Reila
Editing by Gregory F. Augustine Pierce
Drawings by Connie Meyer
Proofreading by Timothy Coldwell

Text copyright © 2024 by Carla Knorowski
Illustrations copyright © 2024 by Connie Meyer

Published by ACTA Publications
7135 W. Keeney Street, Niles, Illinois 60714
(800) 397-2282, www.actapublications.com

All rights reserved. No part of this publication may be reproduced or transmitted in any form or by any means, electronic or mechanical, including photocopying and recording, or by any information storage and retrieval system, including the Internet, without permission from the distributor. Permission is hereby given to use short excerpts with proper citation in reviews and marketing copy, church bulletins and handouts, and scholarly papers.

Paperback ISBN: 978-0-87946-740-1
Hardcover ISBN: 978-0-87946-741-8

Library of Congress Number: 2024948083

Printed in the U.S.A. by Total Printing Systems

Year 30 29 28 27 26 25 24 24
Printing 10 9 8 7 6 5 4 3 2 First

Text printed on 30% post-consumer recycled paper

CONTENTS

Foreword by Michele L. Sullivan / ix

Goodness Gone / 1

Personal Effects / 15

Leaving a Trail / 33

No Room at the Inn / 43

The City of Miracles / 63

Off-Season / 73

Mission Accomplished / 89

The Gift / 103

Epilogue / 111

About the Author / 121

For My Mother, Mary

FOREWORD

Miracles Happen at Every Level

As a young girl attending Sunday school, I was taught many lessons and heard many stories. One story in particular resonated with me: the story of the Virgin Mary appearing to Bernadette Soubirous at a grotto in Lourdes, France.

Bernadette was an unassuming girl, one that history would not otherwise remember. She had a miracle come into her life, and she embraced it wholeheartedly. This paradigm instilled in me a lasting faith and the desire to embrace the miracles in my life as well.

I was fortunate to visit Lourdes and the Grotto of Apparitions in 2014 with my family. The experience was the most touching pilgrimage of my life. People come to the grotto for different reasons. The visit is very personal for most people, whether it is out of curiosity, faith, looking for a miracle, and so on. For some reason, I felt a calling to visit Lourdes and can't explain why. While I was there, I definitely could feel a peace and some kind of a spirit… an overwhelming spirit. The takeaways from my pilgrimage visit were a deep inner peace and the water I collected from the beautiful grotto spring.

Since 1858, the "year of the apparitions," miracles have been documented after visits to the grotto. As a matter of fact, in 2018, the seventieth Lourdes miracle was acknowledged after a paralyzed woman religious was healed after her pilgrimage.

While the Sister's healing was a miracle easily seen, my faith has taught me miracles also happen every day. Not miracles on the level as hers, but smaller ones. I believe it is all how you perceive things. Look around at all of your blessings. Look at all of the events and the people who have impacted your life and how you have impacted others.

In my book, *Looking Up,* **I** write about the influence your perspective has on your life. Miracles

Foreword

happen at every level; your perspective can help you see them.

I've known Carla Knorowski for many years. We met professionally when I was leading the Caterpillar Foundation as its president and she was leading the Abraham Lincoln Presidential Library Foundation as its CEO. Over the years, we have become friends. Through our friendship, I have learned two things about her: She is someone who "looks up" with a vibrant, hopeful perspective and embraces the miracles in her life.

This book tells the story of Carla and her mother, Mary, and how, over time, Lourdes was woven into their intertwined lives, bringing them even closer together in the most beautiful of ways. It is a miraculous journey of reflection, hope, and love; one I know you will enjoy.

Michele L. Sullivan
Punta Gorda, Florida

GOODNESS GONE

They existed.
They existed.
We can be.
Be and be better.
For they existed.

Maya Angelou
I Shall Not Be Moved

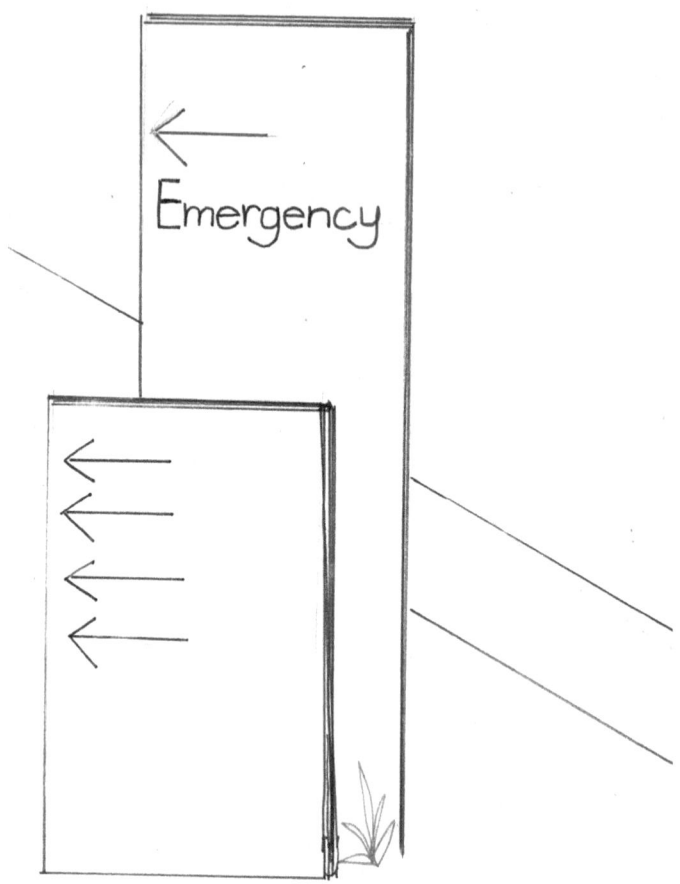

It was the call every child dreads.

"This is Carol from the Grove nursing home. Your mother fell ill and is being taken to the emergency room at St. Joseph's Hospital. She probably should be there by now."

My pulse raced and my heart began to sink. "What happened? Is she talking? Lucid?"

"She was extremely weak, not eating or drinking. But she was speaking."

"Ok, thank you. I'm on my way."

Mom was in her nineties and suffering from vascular dementia, a condition brought on by restricted blood flow to her brain. Her dementia had tricked her into thinking she couldn't walk and that if she tried she most certainly would fall. The first time this happened, her doctors had sent her to the Grove with the hope that the physical therapists would get her walking and help her realize it was matter over mind. She fearlessly accepted the assignment, and each day she did whatever the physical therapist asked her to. In about a month's time, she proudly walked out of the facility aided by her trusty walker.

But dementia had gotten the best of her and again she returned to the Grove. Her world was getting smaller, and she knew it. She became bedridden, but she was determined to live life on her own terms and keep some semblance of control. Dementia might have taken much of her short-term memory and ability to reason from time to time, but somewhere through the fog, as a woman of deep and abiding faith, she knew her most important decision—struggling to merely exist or to let go—was between her and her maker.

I drove as fast as I could, but the trip seemed to last an eternity—each red light feeling more like an hour than a minute. The hospital's façade, which bears a stained-glass mural of St. Catherine Labouré kneeling before the Blessed Virgin Mary, shimmered in the daylight as I pulled into the parking lot. It was reminiscent of St. Bernadette at the grotto of Lourdes—one of my mother's favorite saints. I said a quick prayer to St. Bernadette and went in.

Rushing through the emergency room's sliding doors, I saw walk-in patients resting on their elbows, leaning against walls, and hunched over their knees. An I've-seen-it-all-before attendant sat behind a computer.

"My mother was taken here by ambulance. Mary Knorowski. Last name spelled K-N-O-R…"

I launched in, anxiously awaiting directions from her.

"Room 5. I'll open the door. Her room will be on the right," she directed—unfazed, impervious to any panic, worry, or distress. The locked door clicked open immediately and I was admitted into the ER.

Anxious to see my mother, but fearing the worst, I slid the curtain aside slowly. My immediate fears were allayed. She was awake, seemed to be resting comfortably, and recognized me immediately.

"Oh, Carla," she said looking as if she were crying, but no tears came. She was suffering from extreme dehydration.

I grabbed her hand and returned her gaze. My eyes welled up and my throat tightened. I had seen her only a few days before, but the transformation was shocking. A deep sadness swept over me. Of the many times she had required medical attention, this time looked and felt different. *She* was different. She seemed...ready. "I love you, Mom."

"I love you too, sweetheart," her voice cracking. "You are my one link to goodness."

I took a deep breath, trying to hold it together, overcome by her beauty and eloquence. Her "one link to goodness"? Any goodness I might possess was because of her. I squeezed her hand tighter. While there was no threat of imminent death, it was clear we were saying our goodbyes. We always seemed to be on the same page. Now, not knowing what tomorrow, next week, or next month would bring—if we had that gift of time together—we would leave nothing to chance. Even as we sat in silence, we looked into each other's eyes, connecting in a manner more deeply and richly than we ever had before. And in that fateful moment we knew, we just knew, that the days, hours, minutes, and seconds left to feel each other's warmth, love, and wholeness were fleetingly numbered.

While this was sobering, our relationship was never more beautiful, never more alive.

A hospice nurse once told me that often people, nearing the end of their life, struggle to hang on—more out of concern for their loved ones than themselves. That sometimes they need permission to let go…permission to die. Was this what was happening with my mother now? Somehow, I mustered the courage to say the words I didn't want to say but knew I should: "Mom, you are the strongest person I know, but if you are tired and want to be with Dad, it's okay."

My father, Walter, had died more than a decade earlier. "Please don't worry," I continued. "You and Dad have taught David and me well." David is my older brother. "We want you to always do what is best for you. If you were to leave us, we would be sad and miss you so very much, but you must always do what's best for you."

My mother listened intently. We both knew what this conversation was all about. Allowing death to come. Accepting it. I could hardly bring myself to think the word, but I continued. "Mom, you have blessed David and me beyond measure and prepared us to live happy, vibrant lives. We can never thank you enough.

But now, more than ever, it's about you. Whatever you want for *you* is what *we* want. David and I will be okay as long as you are okay." And then I started to cry.

I said all this while selfishly wanting her never to leave us. Never to leave *me*. Any goodness within me was at odds with my scared and already-missing-her self. She was still living and breathing there before me, yet I felt a cavernous void opening as life's clock wound down our time together. I needed to draw upon whatever courage remained within me and, exhausting that, from my mother, the most courageous person I knew.

Mom had lived much of her life void of any physical illness, yet she had suffered from that quiet, unseen affliction known as "clinical depression." She had experienced two serious bouts during her lifetime. Both times, she was hospitalized. The first, in her forties, occurred when my brother and I were toddlers. She underwent what was then known as electroshock therapy, still a common practice in the 1960s.

For her, however, this cure was worse than the affliction, and she abandoned the treatment. Learning of this in my adult years was devastating. The thought of what she, such a gentle and sensitive soul, must have experienced was all too much to comprehend let alone bear. Given its growing stigma at the time, I could only think of it as adding to her insecurities, anxieties, and self-misgivings. Of course, as a toddler, I knew or could comprehend little of what she was experiencing. But I did experience the loss of not having her there by my side as she sought treatment. I felt a bit bewildered by her absence and stoically missed her—however stoic a toddler can really be—thinking her absence was just a normal part of life. What moms just do.

Mom's second bout occurred in her sixties when she was suddenly laid-off from her job—leaving her and my father, who had already retired, without health benefits in a pre-COBRA, much less pre-Obamacare, America. The stress of that predicament and the thought that she was somehow responsible for it and had failed her family weighed heavily upon her. As a young adult at that point, I watched helplessly as she sat sullenly at family gatherings. One particular time, she seemed almost catatonic, her eyes vacant, even while surrounded by the chitchat and sporadic laughter that came whenever our extended family members gathered together.

Known for her exuberance and distinctive laugh, she sat expressionless in the midst of the cacophony.

Unlike her first bout, this one left its mark. I was sad beyond measure. It left my father bereft. It was the only time I had ever seen him full-on cry. As much as I tried to console him, I knew only my mother's recovery and return home could heal his grief, or mine for that matter.

My mother was our emotional glue. Our light even in her darkness. Our familial compass. When she lost her way, we lost ours. It was gut wrenching to see her physically there, yet mentally somewhere else, lost in a place so deep and dark that it was nearly impossible to imagine her ever finding her way back. Yet she did, somehow, eventually emerging from the abyss stronger than ever before.

When Dad died a few years later in 2003, I feared it would trigger a third and perhaps final bout of depression from which she might never recover. But I had underestimated her. She had become the master of her demons. It was only then that I realized the depth of her courage as she tearfully walked behind my father's flag-draped casket. Then eventually she moved from their home of 50-plus years because aging was making it more difficult for her to perform some of life's simplest tasks. "I don't want to move," she stoically said, "but if I must, I will. Let's get on with it."

Mom moved into an apartment in an independent living facility. Although she would live there alone, she would bring along her books. They were her most intimate friends and constant companions. One, titled *Peace of Soul,* was a gift to her from her beloved sister, who had inscribed it: *To Mary: May you have "Peace of Soul" Love, Julie.*

Another was *Wake Up and Live!* It was her self-help bible. She owned three copies of it—two hardcovers and a paperback—as though no matter when or where she turned, a copy of the book would be within reach… and so too would be some semblance of peace. The book's message? *Act as if it were impossible to fail.*

My mother struggled with her real or perceived failings for much of her life. Once, in discussing them with her doctor, he exclaimed, "Mary, how have you failed? Look at the beautiful, courageous children you have brought into this world and raised! Your son is successfully working and building a life in New York City. Your daughter is off on her own exploring Egypt. You have given them the gift of courage. *Your* courage."

Years later, although she had come to master her demons, she had not vanquished them. And so, even now, *Wake Up and Live!* was often by her bedside. It somehow helped her to stave off or keep at bay the depression she knew lurked in the shadows. Now in her nineties, she and that depression had grown old together. Their relationship was like a wound that had opened and healed, opened and healed, opened and healed so often that there was ample scar tissue—invisible to the eye yet a permanent part of her physiology. While numbing or painful for some, these scars protected and emboldened her. So much so that I had become certain she had been permanently healed. Now, watching her lying in the hospital bed, I knew that my heart was breaking at the realization of her impending death and the life I would soon embark upon without her. It struck me more deeply than I could ever fathom: *My wounded soul will not heal soon, if ever.*

As Mom and I held hands, a flurry of medical personnel rushed in and out of the room. They adjusted cords and PICC lines, took vitals, filled out paperwork. The same questions were asked over and over again by different people. My brother and I knew the drill and patiently answered each. Finally, our mother was formally admitted to the hospital and her condition stabilized. From there she was eventually released, to spend her final few days lovingly surrounded by our family at the home of David and his wife, Janice, both of whom selflessly kept watch, attending to her every need.

Within weeks, Mom took her final breath and, with it, *my* one link to goodness was gone forever. Or so I thought.

REFLECTION

Name a loved one in your life who has died. Read this book with that person in mind.

PERSONAL EFFECTS

"Real isn't how you are made,"
said the Skin Horse.
"It's a thing that happens to you."

Margery Williams
The Velveteen Rabbit

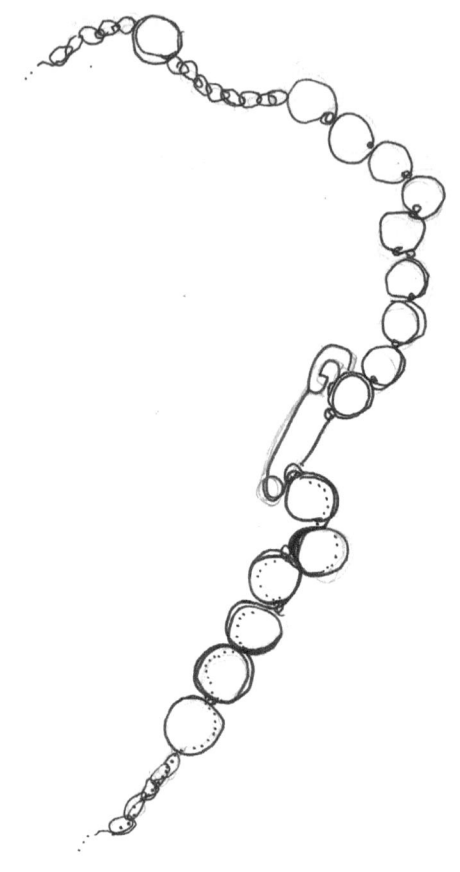

While my mother's death was difficult to accept, I found solace in the memories of our days together, most especially that night in the ER. It was her final gift to me—one more precious than anything other than life itself.

Mom had lived with courage, passion, and purpose—even as death quietly tapped on her door. Now memories were all we had.

Well, memories and her personal effects.

While some may find the task of going through a loved one's things difficult, I find it comforting. Over the years, I have been charged with doing this for many recently deceased family members, including my dad, so the experience was nothing new to me. For me, it is one last opportunity to care for someone I love. It brings me even closer to them. It is a way, albeit after the fact, that I can say "Thank you" and "I love you." It is a way to process my grief.

It was with this perspective that I began to pack away my mother's effects, which included among other things, several devotional items honoring Mary, the

Blessed Mother of Jesus. My mother, a lifelong Catholic, was very devoted to the mother of Jesus. There was a Mary planter with succulents coming out of her back…Mary encased in plastic backlit by a single light bulb…a beautiful replica of a DaVinci masterwork of Mary painted on wood…even an eighteen-inch-high plaster statue I affectionately called "Touchdown Mary" that had been cracked years before by an errant football my brother and I were tossing around the house.

Mary was everywhere, hiding in plain sight. I came across my favorite piece—a white porcelain sculpture of Mary holding the baby Jesus—sitting on my mother's dresser, just as it had for more than half a century. Now I held it in my hand as I sat cross-legged on her living room floor, surrounded by bubble wrap, boxes, and the twenty-five other Marys, large and small, that had been strategically placed originally throughout our home and now finally in her one-bedroom apartment.

As I had done countless times during my childhood, I next pulled out the drawer of her dresser that contained her jewelry collection—tangled strands of beaded necklaces, screw-on earrings, and a few old watches, one with a Speidel-type stretch band. These brought back memories of sleepovers at my cousins' house. As much as I loved going there, each sleepover was preceded by bouts of separation anxiety that I experienced at even the thought of leaving my parents. My mother not only noticed but understood, having battled anxiety throughout her own life.

One night, on the eve of such a sleepover, she came up with an ingenious solution to quell my trepidation. "Here, sweetheart," she said as she removed her silver Timex from her wrist and pulled it over my tiny hand. "I know you want to stay with Mommy and Daddy, but you'll have fun with the cousins. At night when it's time to go to sleep, if you start missing us, I want you to put your ear on the pillow next to Mommy's watch and listen to it ticking. That ticking is just like the sound of Mommy's heart beating. And when you hear it, you will know that I am always with you." As a child, I used to lie there in the darkness of my cousin's house, mesmerized by Mom's words and the thought that I could carry her with me, if only through her watch. And many a night after that, I fell asleep to its ticking—to the beating of her heart.

Tears began to trickle down my cheeks as I held her watch once again and realized the ticking was all I had now... and that it would have to be enough. Filled with sadness over our ultimate separation, I remembered my mother's gentle, calming words. "I am always with you." I dried my eyes, took a deep breath and continued packing the imitation pearls, beads, and baubles she'd loop around her neck—a hodgepodge of colors and shapes.

It was then that I came across it—an indigo rosary she had asked me to get blessed at Lourdes some thirty-five years prior. Sometime in those three-and-a-half decades since, it had lost one "Our Father" bead and five "Hail Mary beads." My mother, however, was never one to discard things, so she had used a safety pin to link the rosary's loop so she could continue to use it in spite of the missing beads. For her, the pin could just as easily represent the six prayers as the beads could. That was who she was and how she thought.

For a fleeting moment, I considered buying some beads and getting the rosary repaired, but I realized it already had been... by my mother...with the pin. This reminded me of one of my favorite childhood stories, *The Velveteen Rabbit*, by Margery Williams, in which an old toy named Skin Horse reveals the importance of not just being old, but becoming *real*: "...by the time you are Real, most of your hair has been loved off, and your eyes drop out and you get loose in the joints and very shabby. But these things don't matter at all, because once you are Real you can't be ugly, except to people who don't understand."

My mother's rosary, like the Skin Horse, was "real." It had been loved by my mother and made real by virtue of that love. It didn't matter that it was missing beads or that it hung awkwardly together by a safety pin. It was *real*. She had made it so, just as she had made me real, and neither I nor the rosary would be "unreal" again.

Gazing upon the rosary, I let it gently fall, bead after bead, decade after decade, from my right to my left hand. It felt almost therapeutic to the touch, soothing both my achy hands and bereft heart. The rosary was so representative of my mother. Her devotion to it and to Mary had been unwavering. Was it because she herself had been named Mary? Was it her ability to relate to Mary as a fellow mother? Could she see in the pure and overwhelming love Mary had for Jesus the kind of love she had for my brother and me?

Or was it much simpler even than that? Something born out of religion or the culture in which she was raised?

From her birth, my mother had been infused with all things Catholic, most especially, the Blessed Mother. As a child, she had learned about the Christian faith and Catholicism through a yearly calendar of faith-based rituals and holy days of obligation. She, like most children raised Catholic, was taught to relate to a bunch of people who had walked the same Earth she was walking, only some two millennia earlier. And she did just that, particularly when it came to Mary of Nazareth.

I sat and wondered, weren't there more modern-day examples from which to learn? That, of course, was where one saint in particular came marching in. It was Bernadette Soubirous, a fourteen-year-old shepherdess from Lourdes, France.

Modern church history records Bernadette as having experienced eighteen Marian apparitions—encounters with the Virgin Mary—during February 11 to July 16 of 1858. Bernadette's story had captured my mother's imagination and heart.

Mom was born the same year Bernadette was beatified by Pope Pius XI in 1925. Later, when my mother was eight years old, Pius canonized Bernadette and officially declared her a saint. For my mother, a child of immigrant Italians devoted to Catholicism and the church, this coincidence with her was extraordinary.

In 1941, when my mother turned "sweet sixteen," *The Song of Bernadette,* a book by Franz Werfel was published and spent a year on *The New York Times* bestseller list. Werfel, a Jewish intellectual living in Europe, had found refuge from the Nazi regime in Lourdes, a town nestled in the foothills of the French Pyrenees. Said Werfel:

> …a family told us that Lourdes was the one place where, if luck were kind, one might still find a roof…we were advised to make the attempt and knock at its gates. We followed this advice and were sheltered at last. We hid for several weeks in the Pyrenean city. It was a time of great dread. The British radio announced that I had been murdered by the National Socialists. Nor did I doubt that such would be my fate were I to fall into the hands of the enemy. It was also a time of great significance for me, for I became acquainted with the wondrous history of the girl Bernadette Soubirous and also with the wondrous facts concerning the healings of Lourdes. One day in my great distress, I made a vow…if I escaped from

this desperate situation and reached the saving shores of America, I would put off all other tasks and sing, as best I could, the song of Bernadette. I have dared to sing the song, although I am not a Catholic but a Jew; and I drew courage for this undertaking from a far older and far more unconscious vow of mine…that I would evermore and everywhere in all I wrote, magnify the divine mystery and the holiness of man.

And so, in commitment to this vow, gratitude for his time there, and for those who most certainly saved his life, Werfel wrote *The Song of Bernadette*, which loosely details the story of Bernadette Soubirous. Two years later, his bestselling homage was made into a Hollywood film of the same name that was eventually nominated for eight and won four Academy Awards including "Best Picture" in 1944. My mother, a voracious reader and moviegoer, was influenced by both the book and the movie, which further fed her love of and admiration for Mary and Bernadette.

In many respects, I was no different than my mother. Being raised Catholic in the 1960s, I learned about Bernadette, who was almost every parochial school girl's super hero. The notion that Mary, the mother of Jesus, would appear not to a priest, nor a nun, nor a boy, but to a fourteen-year-old girl was empowering to me and my female classmates. The Catholic priests and nuns knew it. My parents, especially my mother, knew it. To me, Bernadette's long flowing veil and sash might as well as have been Supergirl's cape.

Born on January 7, 1844, in a millhouse called the Moulin de Boly of Lourdes, Bernadette Soubirous was the daughter of François and Louise Castérot Soubirous. Both parents had dark rugged features, François, clean shaven with squinty eyes framed by high cheekbones, and Louise, deeply set brown eyes topped by thick brows; her hair pulled back and often hidden beneath a traditional Occitan scarf.

Not long after Bernadette's birth, tragedy befell the family when her mother was seriously burned by a candle that had fallen on her as she slept. No longer able to breastfeed, Louise Soubirous had no choice but to send Bernadette to Bartrès, a town two miles north of Lourdes, to be suckled by the thin and wiry wet-nurse Marie Laguës. It would be the first of two occasions Bernadette would be sent to Bartrès and separated from her family.

François and Louise were the children of millers. The Boly mill was part of Louise's dowry. Owned by the Castérot family, the mill was to be both a source of income and the family home, with François and Louise acting as proprietors of the joint establishment. François worked the Boly with its two enormous stone wheels moved by the churning waters of the Lapacca River, a tributary of the *Gave de Pau*, a river that travels through Lourdes to this day. The Lapacca literally flowed underneath the Soubirous' home.

Bernadette referred to the Boly as "the happiness water-mill," as it provided a safe, secure home and steady work for her father. But neither her father nor her mother had the business acumen needed to make a go of it. The family fell on hard times, just about when Bernadette reached the age of ten. Destitute, they would have been homeless were it not for Louise's sister, Bernarde Castérot, and her nephew, André Sajous, who offered the family a place to live in Lourdes' former prison, called *Le Cachot*.

Personal Effects

What must it have been like for Bernadette to be lulled to sleep by the sound of the Lapacca for the first decade of her life, only to later experience the harsh realities of living in a former prison with the stench of a nearby livestock pen permeating the air?

It was *Le Cachot* from which Bernadette happily set out on a clear and mild winter's day in 1858 to collect wood to stoke the family's dwindling fire. Having survived a bout with cholera and suffering from chronic asthma, she often was kept from doing such tasks—things her siblings and friends would do daily as a matter of course. The opportunity to get out of the house appealed to her. Not allowed to go alone, she was joined by her sister Toinette and friend Jeanne Abadie. The three headed to a wooded area with a grotto called *Massabielle* on the banks of the Gave River. Because of her chronic illness, Bernadette was much slower than Toinette and Jeanne, who both ran ahead. All three girls were dressed in frocks, woolen hoods called capelets, typical of Occitan girls at the time. Each wore wooden shoes, but because she was prone to illness, Bernadette, unlike the other girls, wore a pair of stockings provided to her by her mother.

Once there, Jeanne and Marie removed their shoes and crossed the Gave River, hopping from rock to rock until they reached the opposite bank. Bernadette lagged behind and enlisted the help of the girls to help her cross the river. Ignoring her pleas, the girls began picking up firewood, while Bernadette sat down on a rock near the grotto and began removing her stockings. She suddenly heard a "gust of wind" shaking the nearby brambles. Turning in its direction, she spied a "gentle light" emanating from the grotto, which had been immersed in darkness only moments before. Curious, she walked towards it, encountering a "beautiful lady" making the sign of the cross and standing in a nook. Stunned, the teenager fell to her knees and began to pray. It was the first of eighteen apparitions she would experience over the course of six months.

Bernadette would later attest that the "beautiful lady" called herself "the Immaculate Conception." She was too young and lacked the knowledge to understand the meaning or significance of those words and left any interpretations to her inquisitors. Never actually laying claim to having seen Mary, the mother of Jesus, she merely reported what the "beautiful lady" had said or did, including bringing forth a spring of fresh water from the ground where formerly there was none. Bernadette Soubirous' life would never be the same.

Personal Effects

—⋘•⋙—

Such was the story told in Werfel's book and the movie. It was also the story told to my mother as a young girl attending Chicago's Our Lady of Pompeii Church, and it was the story told to me as a young girl studying at St. Genevieve Catholic elementary school and church. While my mother and I were not Bernadette "junkies" per se, on the rare occasions when *The Song of Bernadette* came on television, we would always watch it together.

Back in the 1960s, our television was encased in a boxy, faux-mahogany console. The screen was hidden behind wooden French doors that were meant to be closed when the TV was not in use. When it came time to watch *The Song of Bernadette*, we would throw open the doors as if entering the gates of paradise without leaving the confines of our home. In the case of Werfel's film, we were heading to a foreign land some 1400 feet up in the French Pyrenees.

My mother would sit in a gold upholstered chair in front of the television, while I would sit on the covered radiator behind the couch. It was the warmest spot in the room, and from this vantage point I could see the television on my left, with a wall of my parents' favorite paintings in front of me and my mother on my right. As the film's ominous-then-ethereal score began to play and the words of philosopher-turned-saint Thomas Aquinas appeared on the screen, saying, "*If you believe, no explanation is necessary; and if you don't, no explanation is possible,*" mom and I settled in for our heroine's story, since we were not needing any "explanations." At the time, the film's themes of faith, belief, and redemption were fairly lost on me, but the more sensational, miraculous aspects of the story were not. I was mesmerized, every time.

I was fascinated with Bernadette. This had as much to do with her superhero status as the fact that Jennifer Jones, who played the saintly heroine in the film, was my mother's doppelgänger. She was, at least to me, the spitting image of my mother, whose beautiful chestnut hair, voice, and countenance were like an angel's. What Catholic school girl doesn't believe—or at least want to believe—that she has a saintly heroine for a mom? My mother was this to me, and so much more.

Darkness descended on the room as I finished packing up my mother's things. It had gotten late. My reminiscing had made me lose track of time. I put my mother's watch and rosary in my pocket and headed home. Mentally and emotionally exhausted, I fell asleep to the ticking of her watch.

REFLECTION

**Name one object you have that
you consider sacred.
Read this book with that object close by.**

LEAVING A TRAIL

Go where there is no path
and leave a trail.

Muriel Strode
Wind-Wafted Wild Flowers

International Timetable

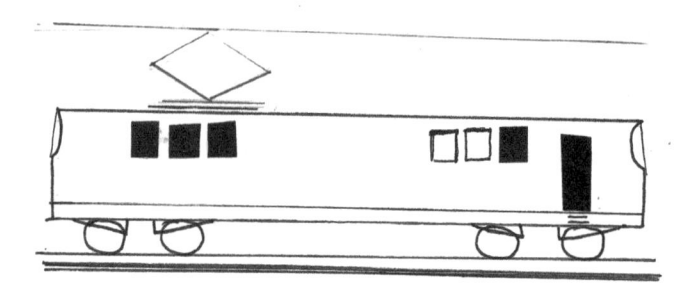

(September, 1982)

The nation was in a recession—what the Federal Reserve called "the worst economic downturn in the United States since the Great Depression." It was 1982, and I had recently graduated from college and was looking for "meaningful" employment (not knowing exactly what that meant). I ultimately landed a sales job at which I was exceedingly successful but not in the least bit fulfilled. Saleswoman was not what I thought I would be when I grew up. Legislator? Perhaps. Journalist? Maybe. But cold-calling saleswoman? Never. I hadn't the panache or grit.

―≪≪◆≫≫―

The job, which revolved around selling fundraising programs to high schools, had me sales pitching coaches, club advisors, band directors, principals, anyone who would talk with a twenty-three year old. While most school fundraisers focused on students hawking candy to sell their way to band camp, the state basketball tournament, or a German Club ski trip, our program focused on selling "decorative" plastic, copper-colored tumblers, each with an embossed winking owl. This decorative accent, we were told, was the key to fundraising success, as owls were supposedly "a popular topic among women." Each time I prepared to deliver my sales pitch, however, I reflected on all the women I knew and none of them, absolutely none of them, were sitting around coffee shops or lunch tables discussing owls...spotted, snowy, or plastic.

I knew innately there was more to life than selling plastic tumblers nobody wanted and would end up in some landfill, but—as distasteful as the job was—I was employed. Keeping this in mind, every day I went to work doing my best to not only make but exceed my sales quota. In addition to the godawful script we were given, we were told to implement a tacky sales technique called "The Pull," which consisted of poking your head into a classroom and motioning by index finger for the instructor to join you in the hall where you'd deliver the sales pitch.

I employed "The Pull" on my first day on the job. I poked my head into the band director's classroom and motioned her out to the hall, her students stopping mid-performance, their musical notes trailing off as if someone had just let the air out of a bagpipe. Much to my amazement, "The Pull" worked! The band director met me in the hall, where I anxiously waited to deliver her and her students to the band camp of their dreams.

Once she learned why I was there, of course, the teacher dressed me down while she rhythmically slapped her conductor's baton in her palm with frightening fury. As her voice reached a crescendo, she threatened that unless I immediately left the school premises, she would have me reported to the principal who, in turn, would undoubtedly have me arrested. No sale was worth this. No *job* was worth this. Apologizing, I made a hasty exit. It seemed "The Pull" was not for the faint of heart, and I never executed it again.

As much as I hated the job, however, it provided income. Still, I was miserable. After five fellow regional directors quit and sales dried up, I decided it was time to join my former colleagues in the ranks of the unemployed.

That very day I booked a flight to Europe with an open-ended return date. I would backpack until I was either too tired to go any further or the meager money I had saved from my job ran out. I was burned out and ready to throw caution to the wind. While I was worried what my parents would say, I decided to risk their wrath for my own health and happiness.

I arrived home to find my father sitting on the living room couch. My stomach clenched. Quitting a job without having another lined up was not something done in our family. It was the moment of truth. His eyes peered over the top of his newspaper when he heard me come in. "Hi, Cark. How was your day?"

Inhaling deeply, I crossed the Rubicon straight into our living room. "Fine, Dad. I made my biggest sale to date, quit my job and bought an open-ended ticket to Europe," I blurted out. "I'm leaving in a few weeks. I don't know when I'll be back." I held my breath waiting to hear his lecture on how I was shirking my responsibilities and needed to buckle down and shouldn't quit a job unless I had another to go to and needed to get on with my career.

Instead, my usually predictable father floored me. "That's great! Good for you. I'm a bit envious. You know how I love to travel," he enthused while I stood there stunned and speechless.

He then folded his paper and laid it down beside him adding. "You know, Cark, your mother and I have been watching you day after day, month after month as you've worked on this job. You've worked hard and showed up every day in spite of how difficult it was for you. We've even noticed you crying at times as you got in the car to go to work. No one should have to work under such circumstances. It was a pressure cooker. Go and have a good time. There will be plenty of time when you get back to find a job and settle into your career." *So much for predictable,* I thought.

I bent down to kiss my dad as tears of happiness began to flow. "Thank you," I whispered. Just then, he added the words that so often ended such moments between us: "Talk to Mom."

My heart raced as I worked out how to reveal my grand plan to her. I paced back and forth in the basement, mustering my courage. Dad was the enforcer when it came to discipline; my mother was in charge when it came to adventure or anything deemed risky. Finally, I walked slowly up the stairs to the kitchen, but before I could utter a word, Mom matter-of-factly asked: "Cark, when you're in Europe, could you please get my rosary blessed at Lourdes?"

She held out her hand, and her indigo rosary dangled from it.

Lourdes? Clearly my mother wasn't aware how off the beaten path Lourdes was (or was she)? An avid reader of poetry and the writings of Transcendentalists such as Thoreau and Emerson, Mom frequently instructed me to go "where there is no path and leave a trail." Perhaps this was my time to do that?

And had I heard right? She didn't say, "*If* you go," but rather, "*when* you go." I stared down at the rosary now in my hands and then back at my mother. My father had obviously broken the news to her and it was a *fait accompli*. Had I been *that* miserable? My sadness *that* apparent? My fingers enfolded the rosary. "Yes, of course, Mom," I responded, a smile bursting across my face. I hugged her as she gently encouraged me, "Follow your heart." She then added for good motherly measure, "Just be careful."

Clearly, I had misjudged my parents, letting fear of what I thought they would say or how they would react get the better of me. I had underestimated the depth of their empathy and love. Watching me struggle with a bad job, both of them had given me enough space to find my own way. Turns out they always did.

While France isn't impossible to traverse, finding my way to Lourdes would take some doing, but that's what a pilgrimage requires. I just didn't know I was going on one or how long it would actually take to get there. But I would drive, fly, take a train, walk, even crawl across France for my mother. And with this conviction firmly planted in my being, I embarked on a journey to Lourdes, determined to "leave a trail."

REFLECTION

What trail have you already left?
What new trail would you still like to leave?

NO ROOM AT THE INN

"This porridge is too salty!"
"This porridge is too sweet!"
"This porridge is just right!"
She ate it all up.

Robert Southey
Goldilocks and the Three Bears

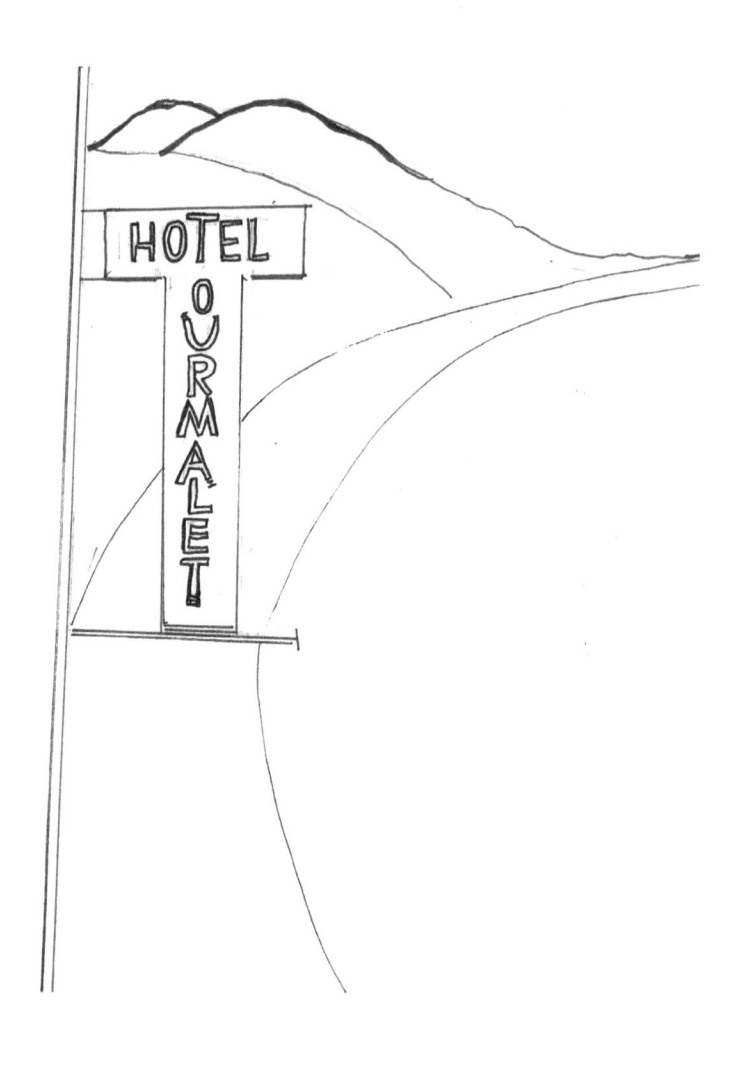

I boarded a plane for Europe and then destinations north, south, east, and west. It was the first week in October 1982. I was free to explore and live life free of conventional expectations. I would satisfy my own, which included getting my mother's rosary blessed at Lourdes.

Landing in Frankfurt, Germany, I donned my brown canvas backpack, which looked somewhat like an enormous russet potato. Another small red backpack rested on my chest, and a pair of hiking boots dangled from a strap, swinging in time as I took my first steps on the journey. I looked like a Sherpa in training but, although I was heading to the Pyrenees, I wouldn't be climbing any mountains.

As the autumn season deepened and hints of winter began to tease the continent, I began moving southeastward, my mother's rosary in tow. There was an air of uncertainty and political change in Europe. Helmut Kohl, the conservative Christian Democrat had just replaced liberal Social Democrat Helmut Schmidt as West German Chancellor. In Poland, Lech Walesa, the Solidarity labor leader, was released from jail, having been incarcerated for his continued fight against the communist state, martial law, and the rule of Polish leader General Wojciech Jaruzelski.

Perhaps the most startling change was one I learned of while traveling on a train from Germany to France, on my way to Lourdes, when a man entered my compartment and opened his newspaper. The headlines declared in German: BREZHNEV IST TOT. Leonid Brezhnev, the face of the Soviet Union for much of my life, was dead. As Nikita Khrushchev's successor, Brezhnev had ushered in détente and a thawing of relations with the U.S. and other nations; but he still ruled with an iron fist. While the consequences of his death left an air of uncertainty hanging over much of the world, I thought about the Soviet Union's promotion of atheism and how Brezhnev and his cohorts might regard Lourdes as a fantasy land. If religion was, as Karl Marx proclaimed, "the opium of the people," I was about to overdose.

I boarded the train which would take me from Paris ever closer to my ultimate destination, Lourdes. But first I had to transfer trains in Toulouse, known as

"The Pink City," where pink stucco and brick dominate the architectural landscape. My plan was to spend one night there and take a morning train to Lourdes the next day. Robert Burns once wrote, "the best laid schemes of mice and men go often askew." (Well, I wasn't a man or a mouse, so I naively and confidently went about my business, trusting the backpacking gods.)

Laying claim to a window seat, I stared through the tinted tempered glass, thinking back on the conversation with my mother that had sent me on this circuitous route to Lourdes. In truth, I was feeling a bit homesick and wondering what might be happening in my absence. Outside, the trees sported a palate of reds, browns, and golds. Back home, leaves were probably blanketing the neighborhood, with the sound of metal rakes scratching the pavement. *Has the first snow fallen in Chicago,* I wondered. Surely by now the city workers were starting to dress the city's street lamps with holiday decorations. What would the Christmas theme be at Marshall Field's this year? Had its traditional tree been put up in the Walnut Room of that store?

I bet myself that my parents were likely preparing to go out to dinner, just as they did every Friday night, followed by a visit to my Aunt Julia's house for dessert.

Maybe she was serving homemade pound cake? Biscotti? Cannoli?

As the train click-clacked through city after city, town after town, I took out my pen and whatever odd piece of paper I had and began to write a letter, as I often did when missing home. This one would be to my college friend Bruce, who was to meet up with me later in the trip. Strangely, it described a portent of things to come:

Dear Bruce,

I'm on a train heading for Toulouse, France. The countryside is really beautiful. The ride is a long one. I'm a little worried because I'll be getting into Toulouse at night and I'll have to find the youth hostel. I've made sure thus far that I always get to a city with plenty of daylight ahead of me, but not this time.

To make things a little more difficult, the train is about forty minutes late. Will I find the youth hostel? Will there be a room at the inn? Will I get lost and end up sleeping on a park bench?

Stay tuned... Love, Carla

No Room at the Inn

After seven hours, the train finally pulled into Gare Toulouse-Matabiau just as the sun was setting. At last, I had arrived in "The Pink City," whose colorful hues were barely observable under a dusky, threatening sky. A smell of rain was in the air. Disembarking, I wasted no time searching for a place to stay. These were not the best circumstances for a young woman traveling alone. My mother's sole directive, "Be careful," was repeating in my head.

Backpackers, by design, rarely book rooms in advance. Not knowing where the road will take you and where you might rest your head for the night is all part of the adventure. But this night, sure enough, I found myself encountering one COMPLET sign after another, indicating there were no vacancies to be found. The youth hostel hadn't a free bed and the *pensions* and hotels I could afford were completely full. Perhaps, as I had joked in my letter to Bruce, I might end up sleeping on a park bench after all. (It wouldn't be the first time.)

I trudged back to the train station to regroup. My backpacks—front and back—were feeling heavier by the minute, and my anxiety was mounting at the same pace. As I approached the station, I looked up at its clock, now brightly illuminated in the darkness of night. Its luminescent hands reminded me that it was getting late. I had to make a decision.

A gaggle of backpackers began gathering just below the clock, and I joined them. We kibitzed over whether to take our chances hanging out overnight in the station or moving on to another destination. The station seemed safe enough and, like most in France, was a work of art unto itself. Minus all its signage, taxi stands, bicycle racks, and loading zones, it might have been mistaken for a chateau. The words CHEMINS DU FER DU MIDI—the name of the original railroad company—were etched just below the clock. The station's façade was adorned with a variety of colorful coats of arms that represented the cities and towns the station first served in the Pyrenees region.

―⋘✦⋙―

Perhaps rather than stay in Toulouse, I thought, *I should pull a round-tripper and sleep on the train for the night.* The round-tripper was a time-honored solution which entailed taking an evening train to some strategically selected outpost about four hours away, then hopping on a return train arriving back just in time for breakfast. It afforded a dry and warm refuge—a safe place to spend the night.

I pulled out my orange-covered *Thomas Cook International Timetable* to come up with some options. Perhaps I could take a roundtrip high-speed train to and from Paris, arriving back in Toulouse late the next morning? Or maybe travel to Tarbes—home of the *Jardin Massey,* one of the best gardens in all of France? Or take a chance and just head to Lourdes, my ultimate destination?

In Goldilocks fashion I ticked down the list:

- *Paris? Too far.*
- *Tarbes? Too close.*
- *Lourdes? Just right!*

It was where I wanted to be anyway, even though I would arrive under the cover of darkness. The smaller the town, however, the greater the chances the hotels would be *"complet"* as they were in Toulouse.

Drops of rain began to pepper the timetable's pages. I had no time to waste and I decided to just go for it. What was there to fear? I was on a divine mission with a rosary in my pocket. I had to have faith that it would all work out.

As I was bidding *adieu* and *bonne chance* to my fellow travelers, a handsome, curly-haired backpacker with dark features and a strong chin approached. He broke into a broad smile and asked, "I'm looking for somewhere to stay. Anyone know a place?" His accent and the blue Union Jack and field of stars sewn onto his backpack told us he was an Aussie. He introduced himself as Adrian from Tasmania. Tasmania? The only thing I knew about Tasmania was the devilish, fanged Looney Tunes cartoon character of the same name.

Adrian, thankfully, looked nothing like him.

His question elicited a sea of groans from the other homeless-for-the-night travelers, and he joined us in lamenting the lack of vacancies. While other options were being bantered about, I blurted out, "I'm taking the 19:03 to Lourdes."

"Lourdes?" Adrian asked innocently. "What's that?"

I gave my Lourdes's elevator speech. Bernadette. Apparitions of the Virgin Mary. Healing waters. I doubted I would get any takers. I mean, Lourdes didn't offer the glitz and glamor of the French Riviera or the merlots and burgundies, champagnes and chardonnays of the French wine country.

All it offered was the possibility of a miracle or two and required a bit of faith or at least an open mind.

A silence fell over the group, when much to my surprise, Adrian responded in earnest, "Really? Mind if I come along? My mum would be impressed."

I laughed and nodded yes. After all, going to Lourdes with a Tasmanian "devil" seemed ironically fitting. Now, no matter what time I arrived I would not be alone. Sure, I would be traveling with a total stranger, but I wouldn't be alone. I smiled, amused by my own irrationality. For all I knew, this stranger might be an axe murderer or serial killer; but, yes, at least I would not be alone.

By my calculations, Adrian was more than 10,000 miles from home. He had left Tasmania only a week prior. He had a fun, carefree air about him. Grounded and down to earth, perhaps because of his "mum's" influence, he exuded warmth and kindness. Anxious to explore, he was ready for an off-the-beaten-path adventure. After all, he was from Tasmania. You can't get more off-the-beaten-path than that.

Trying to put Tasmania in geographical context, I suddenly realized Adrian lived closer to Antarctica than I lived to Los Angeles. It was fascinating. Hailing from a farm town called Broadmarsh, he was one of a population of about 140 people, which was about half the population of sheep.

The town was located at the southern end of one of the world's southern-most islands, bordered by the Indian Ocean and Tasman Sea—two bodies of water exotically distant to me but home to him. It was not quite the end of the earth, but it was close. Yet, there we were, two wayfarers from opposite sides of the globe, brought together by that twentieth-century innovation, the airplane, and the miraculous intelligence, creativity, and innovation of those who had made flight possible.

By contrast, when Bernadette Soubirous wandered the Lourdes region in the 1850s, travel was limited to foot, boat, or horse and buggy. Rail development in France was primarily limited to the north and had not reached the southern Occitan area until the late 1860s. After the Marian apparitions, the demand for transport to Lourdes became so great that the Orléans Railroad Company added a line—no doubt, the one on which Adrian and I now traveled. Bernadette could no more know that humans would eventually take to the skies than she could know that one day, millions of people like Adrian and myself—two likeminded travelers from different hemispheres—would, because of her and her experiences, visit Lourdes.

A shepherd by trade, Adrian was getting a much-needed respite from the *El Niño* Australian drought of 1982—one of the worst in his nation's history. The prolonged period of heat and rainless days led to the massive loss of livestock and catastrophic crop failure. Hundreds of sheep in Adrian's flock perished.

"I helplessly watched as sheep after sheep died," he lamented, staring down onto the metal table separating us as if the solution to such horror might be found written somewhere on its top. "There was nothing I could do." He replayed the experience for me, but the devastating, gut-wrenching nature of it all was unfathomable. I could only sit, listen, and learn. His experience and daily life were so different than the urban life I had lived. And yet we were drawn together through travel—destination Lourdes—where he would impress his "mum" and I would fulfill *mine's* most fervent wish.

Blessing My Mother's Rosary

Even with all this talk of sheep and shepherding, neither Adrian nor I connected the dots—that Bernadette Soubirous, whose world we were about to enter, was a shepherdess. In the year prior to the apparitions, she again had been separated from her family, returning to Bartrès and the farm of Marie Laguës, her former wet-nurse. It was there she lived and tended sheep for reportedly five francs per month. Bernadette's work as a shepherdess afforded her family meager but much-needed income… and one less mouth to feed.

One day, she lamented to her father that "green marks" had appeared on her sheep. Not knowing what this meant, she cried heavyheartedly upon learning from her father that these sheep were marked for slaughter. Like my new friend Adrian, it seemed the shepherdess-turned-saint could not bear the thought of any one of her flock being made to suffer. For me, the thought of watching one sheep die, let alone an entire herd, seemed all too much to bear. But for Adrian, the losses of life and livelihood were dually cataclysmic. Perhaps a year on the road would heal him? Or an unplanned visit to Lourdes?

While this was no walkabout for Adrian, it was the next best thing. Unlike most backpackers traveling from the U.S., Canada or other parts of Europe, those from Australia and New Zealand were hardcore travelers whose journeys usually lasted at least a year.

Aussies also knew how to pack. While I had packed almost all my earthly possessions, Adrian looked like he packed for a weekend at a nudist colony.

As the train sped down the track, he and I became lost in conversation. Before we knew it, we arrived in Lourdes a little after 9 p.m. Fortunately, the Toulousean rain hadn't followed us.

Lourdes, located at the base of the Pyrenees, is at an elevation ranging from 1100 to 3000 feet above sea level, depending on where you are standing in the small town. Judging from the silhouettes of the surrounding hills and mountains off in the distance, it was evident Lourdes was nestled in the foothills. I peered into the darkness imagining what it must have been like in Bernadette's day. It was a mild autumn night—the darkness punctuated by the glare of white neon lights interspersed along the train platform. The solemn silence which engulfed the town was suddenly

Blessing My Mother's Rosary

broken by the squeaking of the train's wheels as it began to roll out of the station. On some level, my arrival there seemed like a miracle unto itself and I wished my mother was with me to experience it—and to get her rosary blessed.

After a quick adjustment of our backpacks, we headed into the station. The *tabac* shops and newspaper stands were closed for the night, as was the information kiosk. We would have to fend for ourselves. Unlike Toulouse, a buzzing urban metropolis, Lourdes was a quiet town with little if any activity.

I consulted Adrian's youth hostel guide, which seemed to list every hostel known to man or at least those in Western Europe. Locating a phone booth, I dialed the number of the nearest one and was promptly greeted by a high-pitched, three-note signal that was immediately followed by a looping recorded message in either French or Gascon—the local dialect. Not knowing either, but recognizing the universal sound of an error message, we knew we were out of luck. Hostels, unlike *pensions* and hotels, didn't provide round-the-clock service. It was just as likely that the phone number was no longer in service as that the hostel owners had gone to bed for the night. Discouraged, I dialed the only other hostel in town. A man answered with a hearty, "*Bonsoir!*" Might we be in luck?

"*Bonsoir,*" I replied then asked, "Is this the youth hostel?"

"*Bonsoir!*" he repeated.

"*Bonsoir!*" I repeated thinking perhaps he hadn't heard me.

"*Parlez-vous français?*" he asked.

"*No. Parlez-vous anglais?*" I asked.

"*Bonsoir,*" he said yet again.

"*Bonsoir,*" I answered.

"*Parlez-vous français?*"

"*Parlez-vous anglais?*"

In this interminable standoff, we suddenly both burst into laughter, as did Adrian. I held out the phone to him, hoping he'd give it a go, but he held up his hands like he was about to be robbed at gunpoint. The Frenchman ended our conversation to nowhere with a few "*au revoirs.*" I "*au revoired*" back and hung up.

Undeterred, Adrian approached a cab driver and inquired about any nearby hostels, to which the cabbie responded repeatedly, "Bar Albert. Bar Albert." This puzzled us. Ask about lodging and get directed to a bar? We dismissed it until a middle-aged woman standing nearby also repeated, "Bar Albert! Bar Albert!" We reasoned that while a drink might calm everyone's nerves, bar hopping wasn't on our radar. We simply wanted a place to sleep. We looked around. There was no Bar Albert nor hostel in sight.

Frustrated, the cabbie drew a cross on a sheet of paper, which, in a place like Lourdes, isn't very distinctive. There are crosses everywhere. He pointed to it saying, "Anglais! Église!" We knew enough French to know he was directing us to an "English church." We thanked him and headed off in the direction he pointed.

With no church in sight, we came across a dorm-like building. From what we could make out, it was some sort of convent or shelter. The building was dark, its doors locked, and our knocks went unanswered. No room at the inn.

As in Toulouse, there was no shortage of hotels in Lourdes but, also like in Toulouse, they all proudly displayed COMPLET signs in their dimly lit windows. Hotel Ste. Bernadette, Hotel le Carillon, Hotel D'Annecy. All *complet*. Then we spotted a hotel off in the distance with nary a COMPLET sign in sight. It was the Hotel Tourmalet. The hotel was named after the *Col du Tourmalet,* a mountain pass in the Pyrenees rising some 8000 feet skyward about an hour southeast of Lourdes. The pass was considered one of the most difficult routes often traversed in the world-renowned cycling race, the Tour de France. After the evening's misadventures and difficulties, it felt as though we were sprinting towards our own finish line of sorts—securing a place to stay for the night.

We were welcomed by a bleary-eyed, slightly disheveled clerk, who looked tired, albeit happy we had arrived. He informed us in broken English that he had one room left, not two. "Only one. Then, *complet*," he said, motioning his arms like an umpire declaring a runner safe at home plate. Then he added, "100 francs with breakfast." Adrian and I looked at each other and replied in unison, "We'll take it." And with that, the COMPLET sign lit up, ready for the next weary and forlorn travelers to read it and weep.

Once in the room, we flopped back on our respective beds. Adrian pulled out two cans of Australian beer he had carried from home. "I was saving them for a special occasion. This is it." We popped the tops, toasted one another, and talked well into the night about everything and nothing. It was as though we had known each other for years. The moment was reminiscent of Frank Capra's Academy Award-winning film, *It Happened One Night,* in which unmarried strangers, played by Clark Gable and Claudette Colbert, are thrown together by chance and end up spending the night together in a hotel room. Scandalous in the 1930s, Capra got around the censors by having the characters sleep in separate beds, but only after Gable hastily hangs a blanket over a rope between them, calling it "the Wall of Jericho."

Adrian may have had Gable-quality looks, but there would be no need for such a wall as we bid each other "G'night." He turned off the light and I lay in the darkness thinking of what and who brought me to Lourdes. *I'm finally here, Mom.* And although she was thousands of miles away, we had never been closer than I felt in the moment.

Tomorrow would be her special day, in spite of Robert Burns.

QUESTION

Bring to mind one person whom you met randomly and then became friends with, even if only for a short time. Think about that person as you read this book; maybe even try to reconnect.

THE CITY OF MIRACLES

Don't gasp at a miracle
that is truly miraculous
because the magic
lies in the fact
that you knew
it was there for you
all along.

Toni Morrison
Beloved

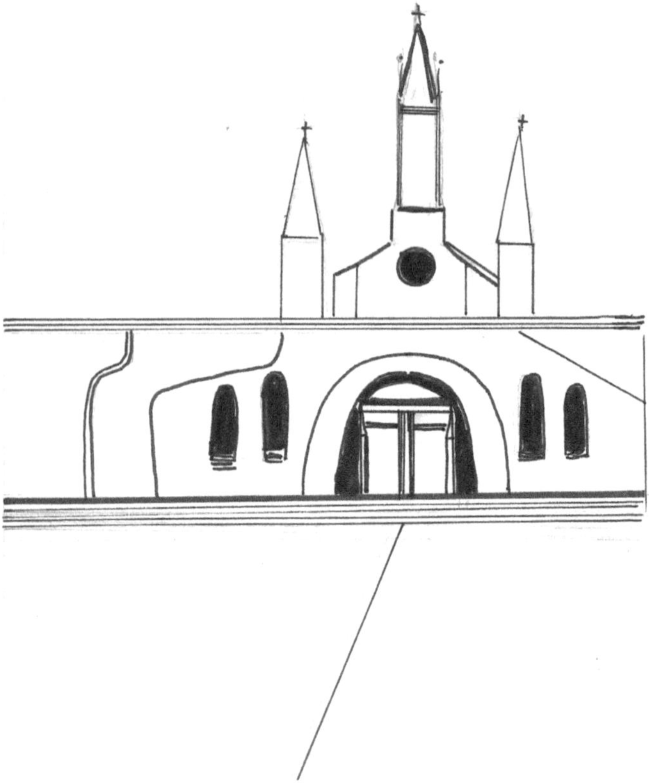

Adrian and I awoke early the next day to the smell of freshly brewed coffee wafting up the staircase. Making our way down, we were treated to a delicious breakfast of coffee, tea, toasted French bread, jellies, and a regionally produced favorite, Tourmalet cheese. For two hungry backpackers on a budget, it was like winning the lottery.

Adrian and I learned over breakfast that Café au Roi Albert—the bar to which the cabbie had tried to direct us—is a restaurant frequented by the millions of globetrotters who flock to Lourdes annually. Referred to as "Bar Albert" by locals, it is a hotspot where English is spoken freely. Located in the old section of town, had we found it, the owners would have undoubtedly directed us to a youth hostel. But we no longer cared; we were enjoying a continental cornucopia of delights at the Hotel Tourmalet.

Having only one day in Lourdes, we were antsy to get moving. After bidding *adieu* to our host, we left our bags and headed to the world-famous Lourdes grotto under overcast skies with a crisp morning chill in the air. The light of day revealed Lourdes as a town that embraced commercialism. I somehow had expected something more reverential and understated, but no. While the Pyrenees cradled Lourdes and its environs like a mother swaddling her newborn infant, the old city center was more like a mother pushing her daughter to sell more macarons as a member of *Les Scouts de France.*

Lourdes was an entrepreneur's dream—a town marketing Mary of Nazareth, the mother of Jesus, Bernadette's "Lady." A glance in any direction revealed a store, café, or hotel with a name bearing some kind of religious reference: Hotel Jeanne d'Arc, Hotel Paradis, Hotel Saint This, or Hotel Saint That. It was so prevalent that I wondered if the city's phone book listings were not only alphabetized, but listed according to Bible chapter and verse. It was disconcerting.

This was not how Hollywood, Franz Werfel, or the Sisters of Providence at my elementary school back in Chicago had described it to me, nor how I had imagined it. I was also sure this was not how my mother imagined Lourdes either.

More than a bit disillusioned, I felt the need to apologize to Adrian, but he just laughed and we continued to the grotto. Surely, I thought, at least THAT would be cordoned off from such commercialism.

The City of Miracles

—⋘✦⋙—

As a child, I had been taught the story of Jesus encountering the money-changers in the Temple. I reasoned that the good people of Lourdes and the owners of the many businesses were technically not inside the temple. So money should be allowed to freely change hands throughout the town. Adrian and I, for example, had been grateful for the hotel and breakfast we had paid for the night before.

Still, the cynic in me wondered if the miracle of Lourdes might be more about the cottage industry of small hotels, bed and breakfasts, cafes, and souvenir shops than Bernadette's sighting of "The Lady" in the grotto. I could easily observe that francs were being made in the names of the apostles and saints, *ad maiorem Pecunia gloriam* (for the greater glory of money), instead of *ad maiorem Dei gloriam* (for the greater glory of God).

We turned down the winding Boulevard de la Grotte, which led us over the Gave River to the front gates of the Sanctuary of Our Lady of Lourdes. Stepping through the gates, I felt like Dorothy entering the technicolor Land of Oz. As in the film, Lourdes' old town, with its black-and-white commercialism, was in stark contrast to the vivid and colorful sanctuary it held at its center and *raison d'être*. This was the Lourdes of my imaginings; of my mother's constant faith. This was the Lourdes she had asked me to visit and have her rosary blessed.

There was nary a money-changer in sight, and Adrian and I were left to ourselves to learn and ponder the meaning of this place of faith, belief, beauty, solitude, reverence, honor, miracles, and how we fit in to it... or not.

My family was not a stranger to miracles, maybe not the kind associated with Lourdes, but minor miracles nonetheless. Back in the 1970s, my mother was a devout listener of *The Wally Phillips Show*, the top ranked radio show in Chicago. "Wally" as he was affectionately called by virtually everyone, held daily contests to engage his listening audience. One time Wally decided to hold a blockbuster contest unlike any other he had previously held. He told his audience that the numbers 51, 33, and 86 were clues to three well-known people. He challenged listeners to name the three and gave them a handful of hints:

The City of Miracles

- Clue 1: Each of the three people is associated with one of three numbers: 51, 33, or 86.
- Clue 2: One is a sports figure.
- Clue 3: One of the numbers is another's age.
- Clue 4: "Here's a clue so you don't get uptight; one is black and two are white."
- Clue 5: "Here's a clue that won't surprise; one's a gal and two are guys."

Listeners could submit multiple entries, and over the course of a few weeks, the station received tens of thousands from Chicago-area listeners. My mother submitted four. Each day as the contest wore on, she would proclaim in true *Wake Up and Live!* fashion, "I'm going to win," acting as if it were impossible to fail. Her family and friends simply smiled behind her back and humored her.

At just after 8 a.m. on July 12, 1971, however, the phone in our brown brick bungalow began ringing. Roused out of sleep, I could hear my mother as she picked up the receiver.

"Hello?" she said in her hoarse morning voice. A brief pause ensued as she listened to the caller.

"Wally Phillips?" she asked with an air of incredulity.

Wally Phillips? Could it be? Did Mom actually win? I shot up straight in my bed, listening intently to her one-sided conversation.

"Oh, Wally!" she exclaimed, her voice cracking as if she were about to cry.

And who would blame her? Wally Phillips, "playing Santa Claus" had just proclaimed her "the smartest woman on West Oakdale—maybe in Chicago" informing her that she had "won it all—the whole marble bag!"

With only five clues, my mother had miraculously solved the puzzle:

- 51 was Chicago Bears linebacker Dick Butkus's jersey number.
- 33 was television comedian Flip Wilson's birth year (1933).
- 86 was the sum of British model Twiggy's combined measurements (31-23-32).

My mother and her brilliant, creative mind had figured it out. Wally proceeded to read off the list of items she had won:

- a savings account at the Bank of Albany Park,
- a SKIL power tool,
- a gift certificate from Republic Lumber Market,
- $14 worth of paint from True Value Hardware Store,
- 10 LPs for her record collection,
- a gift certificate from William A. Louis clothiers,
- a Rival can opener from Wieboldt's Department Store,
- a case of Miller High Life beer,
- some Perfect Plus panty hose,
- some PFD laundry detergent,
- a Norbert pool for the kids,
- a dinner for two at the Stockyard Inn,
- a brand-new beautiful Subaru automobile!

While some might call it luck, fate, or playing the odds, my mother called it "a miracle," and she was right. She had submitted only four entries and her first proved the winner.

Now, almost two decades after my mother's tiny miracle, I was walking through the City of Miracles, driven to go there by a woman whose faith, optimism, and love were miracles unto themselves.

QUESTION

What is the closest you have come to a true miracle in your own life? Bring the memory to mind and recall it as you read this book.

OFF-SEASON

All things have their season,
and in their times
all things pass under heaven.

Ecclesiastes 3:1

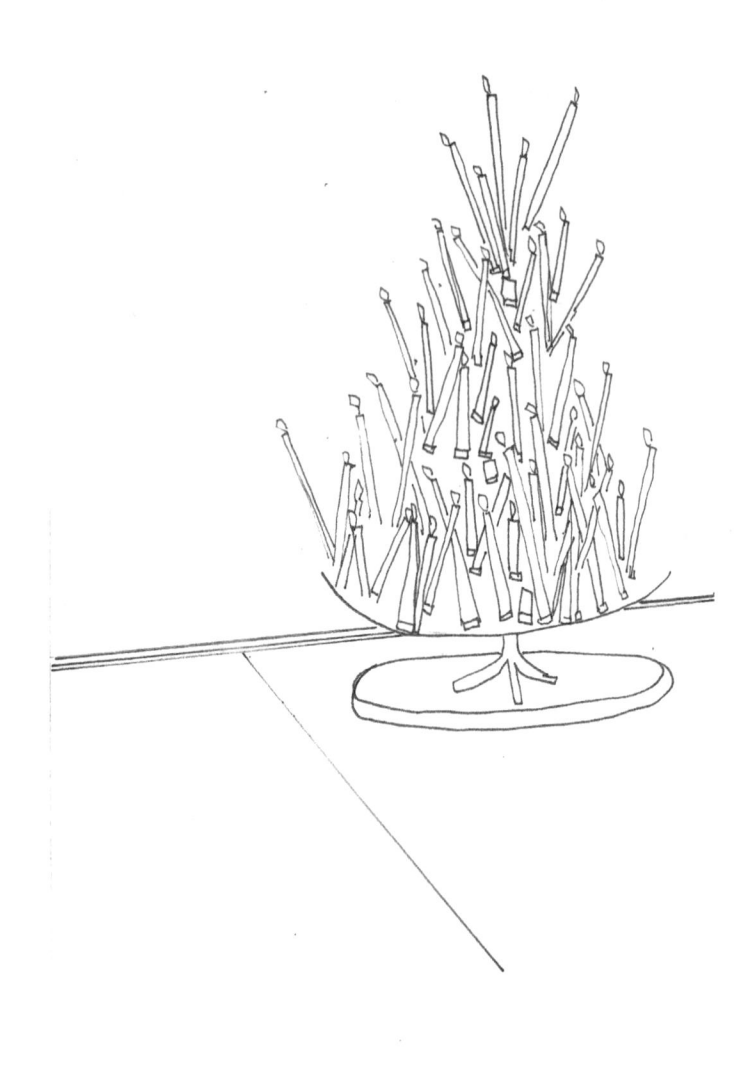

Adrian and I wandered down the expansive *Esplanade des Processions* into the *Esplanade du Rosaire* and directly to the grotto. The majestic *Basilique Supérieure,* also known as the *Basilique de Notre-Dame de l'Immaculée-Conception* (the Basilica of Our Lady of the Immaculate Conception), rose before us like a flower-bud sprouting towards the heavens. We had the space virtually to ourselves. (In the summer months, it would be teeming with millions of international pilgrims, but this was the off-season. Apparently, even a shrine can have an off-season.)

If the esplanades could talk, the stories they would tell, I marveled. For all the curious tourists who visited Lourdes, there were millions upon millions who came for more serious reasons. They came on gurneys or in wheelchairs, hobbling on crutches or limping with canes. A few were healed, (there is little argument about that); most were not, (there is no argument about that). And still, they came. They came deaf or blind, bearing physical deformities, diseased with hidden maladies such as cancer, diabetes, leukemia, AIDS. They brought their struggles with autism, dementia,

Down syndrome, anxiety, depression, addiction, loneliness, grief.

They were 124-years' worth of mothers, fathers, daughters, sons, sisters, brothers, aunts, uncles, cousins, neighbors, friends, co-workers; 124 years of bus drivers, teachers, machinists, engineers, homemakers, doctors, lawyers, cobblers, builders, students, priests, vowed religious, laypeople; 124-years of pilgrims, believers, non-believers, Christians, non-Christians, agnostics, and even curious atheists.

They were shepherdesses like Bernadette and shepherds like Adrian. They were famous, infamous, anonymous or forgotten. They came from near and far, hoping to experience something miraculous.

―⋘✦⋙―

We walked to the entrance of the *Basilique Supérieure*, an extension of the grotto. The enormous structure loomed large before us. It was designed by architect Hippolyte Durand, who had studied at the famed École des Beaux-Arts in Paris. Durand had made his mark designing grand homes for Napoleon Bonaparte and author Alexandre Dumas. Also an expert in religious architecture, he served many

French dioceses throughout his career building or restoring a number of churches.

The groundbreaking for the Lourdes basilica took place in 1862, just four years after Bernadette experienced the apparitions and the same year when, after a long inquiry into the veracity of her claims, Monsignor Laurence, the Bishop of Tarbes, officially declared the appearances as "certain" and bearing "the distinctive marks of truth." The basilica was built just above the grotto—the site of the apparitions. It was completed in 1871 and consecrated in 1876. It stands, as it has for almost a century-and-a-quarter, as one of the most visited shrines in the world.

Although constructed in the nineteenth century with stone quarried in Lourdes, Durand designed the basilica's edifice in more of a thirteenth-century gothic style. Three spires balance the façade, with the largest in the center rising from the ground to the height of a twenty-six-story building. At the center of the spire is a clock, and every fifteen minutes it chimes "Immaculate Mary," the Marian hymn written especially for Lourdes's pilgrims by French priest Jean Gaignet in 1873. Two ramps, set off with statues of apostles and saints, are located on either side of the basilica. They form the shape of a heart and lead to the building entrance. In front of the doors are an enormous gilt crown and cross. Equally enormous is the stained-glass rose window gracing the entrance above the doors.

Throughout my life, I had imagined Lourdes as a building-free sanctuary. For me, Lourdes was the grotto, only the grotto. Still, seeing the basilica wasn't surprising to me. It was what "The Lady" had instructed in Bernadette's thirteenth apparition: "... build a chapel here." The basilica is more than a chapel, it is an extension of the grotto itself. As I gazed upon the magnificent structure, its spire soaring skyward, I sent a silent message, *I'm here, Mom. Today, your rosary will be blessed.*

Adrian and I entered the basilica, taking in the lovely stained-glass windows that depicted Old and New Testament stories of the Immaculate Conception. He began his brief walkabout, while I pulled out Mom's rosary. Unlike the many other churches, basilicas and cathedrals I had already visited on my trip to enjoy the architecture, statuary, and artwork, this visit had a greater purpose.

Looking at the rosary, I was suddenly transported back to the Sundays I experienced at St. Genevieve Church in Chicago, named after the patron saint of Paris. I replayed in my head a scene I witnessed quite often when I was a child. My mother, Mary, kneeling in her favorite pew, saying the Rosary.

The beads of the rosary dangling from her delicate hands were indigo—the color most often associated with the Blessed Virgin Mary's mantle of blue—that signified heavenly skies, mystery, and peace. As my mother moved her thumb and index finger from bead to bead, the rosary would gently sway and brush ever so slightly against the wooden pew, making a distinctive sound. Whenever she let me hold the precious strand, I tried to mimic the ritual, but my tiny fingers were not as nimble. Invariably the noise I produced, slapping rather than brushing the rosary against the pew, startled churchgoers and prompted heads to turn and a few side-eyed glances to be leveled in our direction. Not missing a beat, my mother would take back the rosary, but not before she stroked my hair to convey that she was not angry. She would then continue her prayers.

The rosary had a healing, calming effect on her. Often, I spied her large brown eyes well up and a few tears find their way down her cheeks which she would gently wipe away. Unlike worry beads, which satisfy the nervous or bored, the rosary's spiritual meaning and my mother's connection to it were deeply fulfilling to her. It healed her in ways no pill or tonic ever could. After Sunday Mass, she would return the rosary to a small brown change purse and, once home, remove it from its pouch and hang it over the upper righthand corner of her dresser mirror. Another rosary, with a gold centerpiece and crucifix hung there as well. While it was much fancier than the indigo one, my mother used it far less than the one I now carried to Lourdes.

Understanding how she loved it so, I was honored she had entrusted me with it. Looking at it more closely, I saw that "Roma, Italy" was imprinted on the back of its silver crucifix. My mother, who was fluent in Italian, had never been to Italy. Had her parents, who emigrated from a small town north of Rome, brought it from their native land? Could it be my grandmother's rosary now making its return trip to Europe? Like the Vatican-prescribed Joyful, Sorrowful, and Glorious Mysteries of the Holy Rosary prayer, all of which revealed the story of Christ's life through the Gospels, my mother's rosary was a mystery unto itself.

Off-Season

While admiring its detail as I sat in the basilica, I examined the rosary's centerpiece, which joined together the main loop of beads to the crucifix. Unlike other rosaries I had seen that had a solo image of Jesus or Mary, this one had a young girl praying to Mary. I turned it over and realized the centerpiece was a receptacle with the words *"eau de Lourdes"* written on it. I smiled. It contained water from Lourdes. The young girl on the front of the centerpiece was Bernadette, praying to Our Lady of Lourdes at the grotto. My mother's request to have her rosary blessed at the shrine made even more sense now. The rosary, in a sense, had come home.

It was just like my mother not to point out the connection. She wanted me to find out for myself. Exploration for her went way beyond travel. To her, everything was a joyous mystery meant to be explored whether it was the contents of a book, a new recipe, or a museum. There was an insatiable curiosity intrinsic to her being. No doubt, she wanted me to explore not just Lourdes, but the rosary itself. I supposed there was no better place to discover this than in the sanctuary steps away from the grotto where the water flowed abundantly. I chuckled, imagining my mother winking at me, lifted my head, pocketed the rosary, and went to catch up with Adrian.

"Do you like it? Where were you?" I inquired.

"I was looking about for a priest to bless the rosary. Couldn't find anyone."

Try as we might, neither of us could. Apparently, off-season was truly off-season. Somehow, I thought it would be like the Cathedral of Notre-Dame in Paris, where there was always a priest on duty sitting in a dimly lit side nave, available to talk with visitors whether they sought spiritual guidance, wanted something blessed, or were just seeking information about the cathedral. Surely, we would find a priest in the sacristy. We went back into the church and I peeked into where the priests dress for Mass, feeling like an intruder; but the room was empty.

We next made our way to a smaller, more modest prayer chapel called the Chapel of Adoration. As we entered, we were purposefully led by its design down a narrow tunnel-like hall, where only a handful of pews were visible in front of the altar, which bore a gold monstrance or *ostensorium* displaying a consecrated Eucharistic host, its sacred contents on perpetual adoration.

Off-Season

As a child, the monstrance scared me, perhaps because the word sounded so much like "monster." I imagined that whatever it was, it could not be good. There was also a secretive nature surrounding adoration that increased my anxiety tenfold. At our parish, the monstrance was rarely put on display and the nuns spoke about it in hushed voices. I wondered if we all might be blinded if we looked at it too long with our impure hearts. This image was only underscored when the nuns lined us up in military fashion to view it. My classmates and I knew the punishment for any unruly behavior was upped substantially whenever the monstrance was on display.

With nary a nun or priest to be found, Adrian and I walked out towards the rushing Gave River flowing the length of the sanctuary. If we couldn't find a priest, we reasoned, we would bathe the rosary in the spring's sacred waters. It couldn't hurt.

We first walked beyond the grotto to look in the baths where pilgrims experience the healing, icy spring waters. The area was vacant except for the carts used in-season by the *brancardiers* (stretcher-bearers) who transport the infirm not only to and from the baths and destinations throughout the sanctuary, but also to and from the town's train station and nearby accommodations. The carts, now empty, were lined up waiting for another season of pilgrims, who typically came in the warm-weather months of early April to late October. We were there, basically alone, in November, but it didn't matter. We were undaunted.

Doubling back to the grotto, we were surprised to see an altar at its center. While I imagined it would be quite an experience to attend Mass there, it seemed out of place in the natural setting and in fact blocked the full visual experience of the grotto. Apparently, the grotto had been altar-less until 1958, when the current one was placed there in honor of the centennial anniversary of the apparitions.

Immediately to the altar's right was a gigantic candelabra, about ten feet high, which looked like an enormous Christmas tree made of white candles. There were about ninety of them of varying sizes, some as large as two feet in height and as thick as a half-dollar. All ablaze, the candle tree's base was covered with a mound of wax drippings, the remnants of melted candles and, I imagined even more so, melted prayers. I learned later that up to four hundred tons of wax are cleared annually from the tree's base. *Futiers* keep watch over the candelabra seven days a week, twenty-four hours a day, insuring there is always a full complement of lit candles.

My mother loved candles. She kept a glass votive candleholder on her dresser. It was set in an ever-tarnished, sterling silver base with sculpted images of the Virgin Mary, Jesus, and four other saints carved into it. When she lit it, the candle's warm glow would shine through the red glass, mimicking votive lights in most Catholic churches. Leaning against the mirror behind the candle was an array of Italian funeral cards memorializing deceased family members, friends, and extended *paisanos* who had passed on. Most frequently memorialized was her mother, whom she affectionately called "Ma." The last details of her mother's life could be found printed on four cards, each depicting a different image: the Crucifixion, Jesus and Joseph, Jesus the shepherd tending his flock, and the Virgin Mary appearing at Fatima, all asking God to conduct her mother to a "place of refreshment, light, and peace."

Now, looking up just beyond the candle tree, the image of the Blessed Virgin Mary rose up before us, reminiscent of one of my mother's cards. It was a statue situated in a nave at the precise location Bernadette identified as where "The Lady" appeared to her.

The statue, made of Carrara marble, was sculpted by French sculptor Joseph-Hugues Fabisch. It depicts Mary with her eyes gazing slightly upward toward heaven, a rosary draped over her right forearm, her hands clasped in prayer. She wears a white gown with a traditional blue sash. Fabisch tried his best to base his work on the discussions he had with Bernadette in September 1863 in which she conveyed to him how the Blessed Virgin had appeared to her. Unfortunately for the sculptor, as history recounts it, Bernadette thought his work beautiful, but not representative. Still, the statue remains the chosen placeholder for the Blessed Virgin Mary, dedicated on April 4, 1864. It is considered Fabisch's most well-known work and joins Michelangelo's "Pietà" and "David" in the pantheon of Carrara marble masterworks.

Inscribed just below the statue are the words, "*Que soy era Immaculada Councepciou*" ("I am the Immaculate Conception") written in the local Occitan dialect. These were the exact words Bernadette revealed Mary had said to her. Foliage had grown around the nave and, although it was mid-fall, it was still green. Adrian and I could only imagine how beautiful the area must be in the warmer seasons when the grounds were in full bloom. But this was our-season, and we would make the most of it with or without a priest.

QUESTIONS

What makes a space sacred? What is the most sacred space you have experienced in your life to date? Keep that place in mind as you read this book.

MISSION ACCOMPLISHED

Sometimes wholehearted commitment
leads to the most meaningful of outcomes.

Mark Lawrence
The Liar's Key

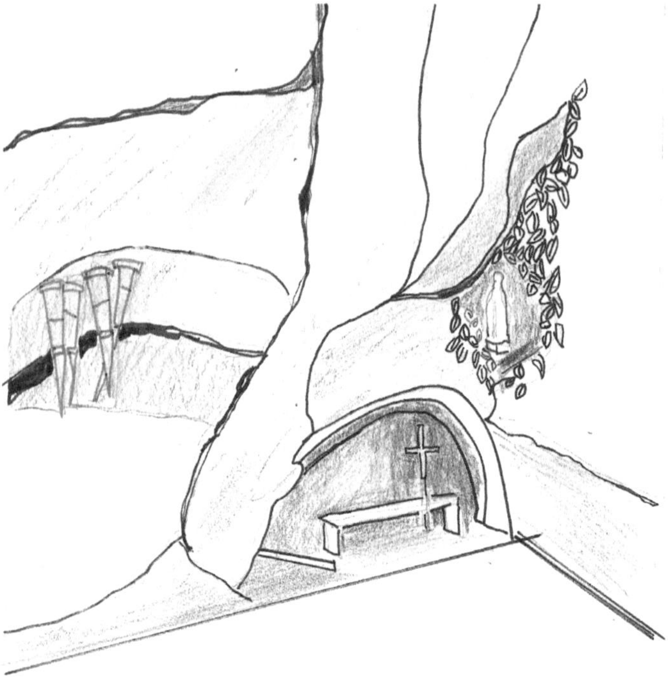

As we stood at the grotto, I spotted a basket in which visitors could drop written prayer offerings and special intentions. I quickly searched for something to write on, but all I could find was a business card. I began scribbling down the names of family members and friends—putting forth one all-encompassing intention on their behalf. My most special intention, the one I singled out, was for my godmother, Aunt Mary, who had been wheelchair bound for as long as I could remember. This was due to rheumatoid arthritis.

I had heard stories of how Aunt Mary loved to dance, but her dancing days had ended long before I was born. From my earliest days, I remembered her assisted by either a cane, a walker, or a wheelchair. Still, she danced with her heart. She had an undeniable vibrance and sense of humor. She loved to laugh and make others laugh as well. While the arthritis was physically afflicting her body, her mind was free from illness or malady. Perhaps that is why my mother loved her so. My mother, on the other hand, had the blessing of physical health, but at times struggled with anxiety and depression. She would often lean on the armrest of Aunt Mary's wheelchair and the two would talk for hours. These two Marys gravitated toward each other because they could relate to affliction both seen and unseen. They were compatriots, finding miracles in each other and not giving in to the illnesses which tried, but never could, enchain or claim their souls.

These were the enduring images that dashed across my mind as I dropped my business card into the intention basket. In addition to the card, I left behind a small piece of my heart as I longed for both Marys and the home I had left behind just a few short months earlier. Adrian followed behind me and although he didn't leave an intention—I had (and still have) no clue of his religious leanings if any—he respectfully watched in reverence. Other backpackers might have long since made a hasty retreat to a nearby pub or to catch the next train out, but Adrian had committed to experiencing Lourdes and remained true to that commitment.

I turned my attention back to the grotto, which created the illusion of being split in two. Half of it was covered in foliage; the other half was bare white-gray Pyrenean stone. Opposite Fabisch's statue were about twenty nineteenth-century wooden canes and crutches. Once a necessity for their owners, they were seemingly discarded after their owners had been miraculously cured through faith, prayer, or an encounter with the grotto's healing waters. While the sight of them undoubtedly gives hope to the infirm who visit, there is something eerie about them. Who were the owners of each? What were their stories?

Not all who were cured of their maladies were lame, of course. The first of the recorded miracles there was experienced by Louis Bouriette, a laborer from Lourdes. He had been injured in a mining accident in 1839 that damaged his right eye and eventually led to his loss of sight. Later in his life, he began visiting the grotto and bathing his eye in the spring while praying to the Blessed Virgin. After a relatively short period of time, his sight was restored and he was proclaimed cured. This was confirmed by a medical doctor to the commission that had been set up at the time by Monsignor Laurence to review all claims of miracles. In 1862, the commission declared Bouriette's healing a miracle of a "supernatural character."

Like Bouriette, my mother had lost the sight in her right eye. As a youngster, she was playing with friends when a stone shot out from under a bike's tire landing near a young boy from the neighborhood. Thinking she had thrown it at him, he picked it up, flung it at her, and shattered the right lens of her glasses. Tiny shards of glass rendered her blind in that eye.

Unlike Bouriette, the accident also left my mother with a severe case of strabismus—an extremely crossed eye. The stone had shattered more than her glasses, it shattered her self-confidence, making her self-conscious and adding to her insecurities. But, through the miracle of science, she was fitted with an artificial eye. Although still physically blind, the strabismus was gone. As she recounted, she could look at herself in the mirror believing, "I'm beautiful again!" (To my mind, Mom was perhaps too young to understand and too blind to see that she always was and always would be beautiful regardless of any malady which might befall her.)

And she was made even more beautiful through the miracle of forgiveness. Shortly after the accident, my mother and her family attended a neighbor's wedding. The young boy who had thrown the stone was also in attendance. Noticing the boy and his parents, my grandfather approached their table. Many of the wedding-goers, including my mother, nervously watched, fearing an argument or physical altercation might ensue. But Mom later told me, "Pa" as she affectionately called him, "wrapped his arms around the boy to console him. He knew the young boy hadn't meant to blind me."

Throughout her life, my mother never let her eyesight hold her back or give her cause for bitterness, resentment, or vengefulness. While she had lost the gift of full sight, she gained the gift of forgiveness in its purest and most powerful form. Bouriette's miracle came when his sight was regained; my mother's when her sight was lost.

And so, with an everlasting faith in all things being possible, I took out the rosary and bent down to the spring flowing from the back of the grotto. The water bubbled up, just as it had for 124 years. I submerged the rosary and then held it in the palm of my hand and prayed: *Bless this rosary and my mother who loves it. May it bring her continued happiness and, when she encounters dark times, may it bring her courage and strength. Thank you for blessing me with such a wonderful mother and family and for the opportunity to travel. Bless our family and please watch over Adrian and me as we travel and go our separate ways.*

In my teenage years, I had been a bit of a recluse when at home, staying in my bedroom rather than spending time with family. This prompted my father and mother to start calling me "the door" because my bedroom door was always closed and I was behind it. Now, my mind flooded with the faces of my parents, family, and friends and the deep and abiding love I had for all of them. I missed them and was learning with each passing day that the old cliché, "absence makes the heart grow fonder," was true. I wished my family and friends were physically there with me at Lourdes to share in the moment.

But my newfound friend, Adrian, was waiting patiently, and so I dried off the rosary and returned it to my traveler's belt for safekeeping.

"What did you put in the basket?" he asked.

"My business card. I had nothing else to write on. I wrote some intentions on it."

Adrian nodded his approval.

"Using a business card felt a little tacky, like I was throwing it into a fish bowl at a restaurant," I said. "Who knows, maybe I'll win a chicken dinner for two at Bar Albert!" We both laughed, cutting the air of solemnity that surrounded us.

Mission Accomplished

Adrian walked over to a wall of spigots out of which the sacred waters could be bottled for easy transport. The first spigots appeared on the site on April 14, 1858, about six weeks after the spring appeared. We each pulled out our water bottles and began filling them when Adrian placed his boot-clad feet under the spigot. Water fell onto the toes of each boot trickling off in various directions.

"What are you doing?" I asked. It was still quite brisk out, and walking around with wet feet was the last thing a backpacker wants. But Adrian had other ideas.

"I've got a year's worth of trekking ahead of me. Thought I'd have a go." His twinkling eyes glistened and his confident smile stretched from one sideburn to the other.

Whether or not Adrian believed in the sacred powers of Lourdes and its water, he clearly was taking no chances. Some aspect of the place must have stuck with him to lead him to this impromptu foot bath.

"Great idea!" I exclaimed, letting the icy water pour onto both my feet. *Bless us… bless our travels and bring us safely home,* I silently prayed, as Adrian drank a bit of the water from his cupped hands.

If anything is the perfectly transportable symbol of faith and hope, perhaps it is the spring water that flows from the grotto at Lourdes, the source of the fountains just steps away and the water still flowing freely. Commercially bottling the sanctuary's fresh spring water would be a distributor's dream, but it is not allowed.

Sourced from springs all over the world, water has a long association with religious themes, from Source Cachat, once known as the Saint Catherine Fountain in Évian-les-Bains, France, to "Sanctuary" Spring in Rodney, Michigan, in the United States. One need only walk through the historic section of Lourdes to know that bottle producers alone are making a fortune selling empty containers to the millions of pilgrims who annually flock there. While the Roman Catholic diocese serving Lourdes freely offers the grotto water to those visiting the shrine, it has been known to be sold by the occasional visitor looking to make a buck. This practice is severely frowned upon. Adrian and I were grateful to have one bottle each filled with the life-affirming water as we continued on our respective journeys.

We both knew our time together was winding down. We began to make our way to the exit.

On the road you tend to get to know people more quickly. Your guard is down and you can talk openly about almost anything—from politics to family, from *El Niño*-triggered droughts to rosaries and Marian shrines. This makes parting all the more difficult—at least for me—even if on-the-road encounters have been brief and transitory. They are still memorable and fulfilling. But in this case, the goodbye was even more than that.

"Adrian, before you go, I have a book I'd like you to sign. "You could write a message if you'd like," I sheepishly said, pulling out the faux-leather-covered black book and handing it to him. I had a tradition of having my fellow travelers sign and leave a message in the book as a memento of the person and the time we spent together.

"Sure!" he said without hesitation. I stood there like an enamored fan waiting for an autograph. He wrote:

20th Nov.

Dear Carla,

From your traveling buddy between Toulouse and Lourdes. Great to meet up with you – will catch you again one day.

Your mate from Down Under: Adrian
"Haere mai" Broadmarsh Tasmania.

Clap! went the book as he snapped it shut. Handing it back, he looked on as I read it.

"What does *Haere mai* mean?" I asked stumbling over the pronunciation.

"It's a local Māori expression we use. It means 'welcome.' You are always welcome in Broadmarsh, Carla," as he flashed his megawatt smile.

"Perhaps," I said with a long pause, "that will be our next meeting and the beginning of another great adventure."

We made our way to the train station. It was time to move on. We hugged each other and after a kiss on each cheek in our best French style, we bid each other safe travels and headed for our respective trains. Adrian would head southeast toward Egypt and I would head a little closer south to Spain.

Such is life on the road. Two people brought together for a few minutes, hours, even days then suddenly off in different directions, fading into the distance, leaving you to ponder: *I wonder whatever happened to….*

No matter how brief our encounters, I hoped that Adrian and all those I had met along the trip would experience some measure of *happily ever after.*

QUESTION

Who is an "Aunt Mary" in your life? Keep that person close in your heart and mind as you finish this book.

THE GIFT

My mother really loved me.
And one of the gifts
that I have been given
is that I have never thought
for one second of my life
that I was not greatly beloved.

Mary Gordon
Circling My Mother

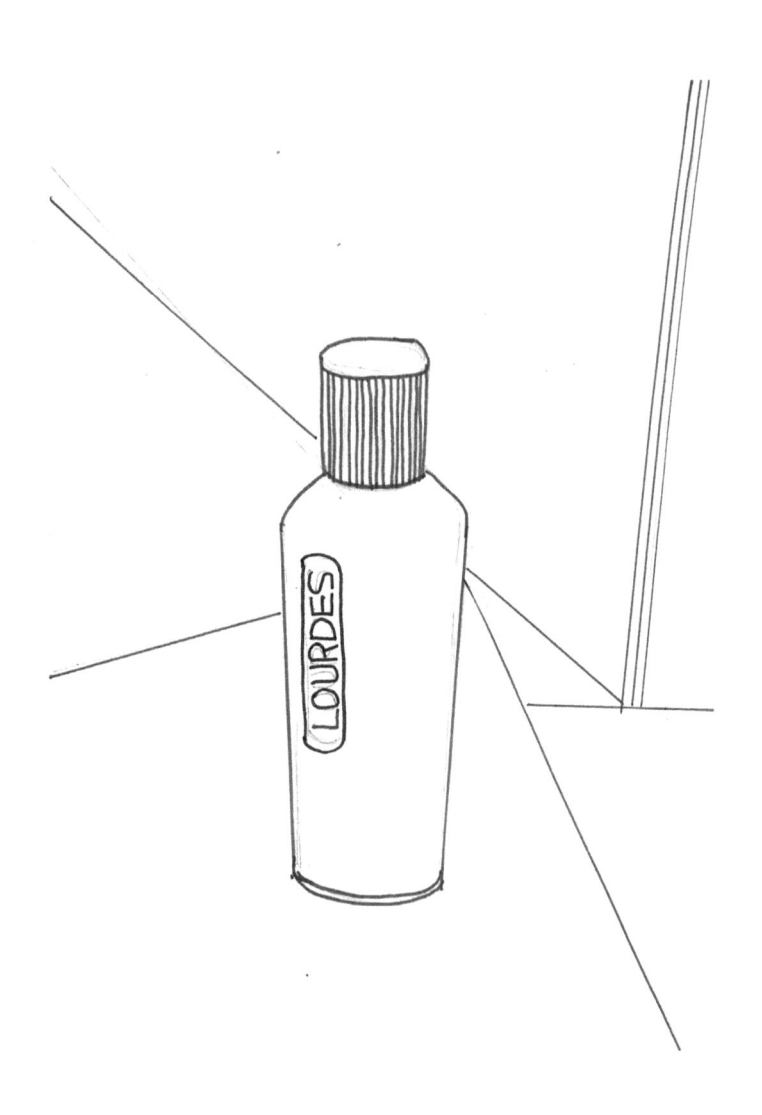

Solo again, I climbed aboard the train that would take me back to Toulouse, on to Narbonne, and from there to Barcelona. The conductor's whistle sounded like a play being called dead on a football field. I could hear the train's heavy steel door slam shut and its wheels slowly starting to turn. The Gave River rushed in the distance below the track's embankment and the large expanse of the sanctuary lay before me, the grotto and basilica rising out of the Pyrenean rock. I bent down and grabbed my camera, but when I looked up, it all was gone. Another fleeting, dreamlike moment had passed.

I pulled a postcard out of my pack to drop a note to my mother and let her know I had in fact reached her hallowed destination. On some level, she must have asked me to go to Lourdes half-thinking I would never get there, that I would become preoccupied with sights of Paris and elsewhere and simply run out of time. When it came to living our lives, Mom always emphasized to my brother and me that we should take responsibility for our own choices and not do something we didn't want to do just because someone else was asking. Or, still worse, because we were being pressured to do it. In her mind, going to Lourdes was a favor she had asked of me, but it was up to me whether or not I would fulfill her request.

My mother keenly understood the fallibility of humans: If anything, we are consistent at being inconsistent; reliable at being unreliable. And even the most consistent and reliable among us still have momentary lapses. This is precisely the reason why my annual New Year's resolution is always not to have one. (It is the only resolution I know I can keep.)

I stared down at the Lourdes' postcard, hoping it would be a visual confirmation for my mother that I had gone there because I *wanted* to go. Its front featured a photo of the grotto, altar, statue of the Blessed Virgin Mary, and candelabra—the exact spot Adrian and I had stood only hours earlier. Across the upper left-hand corner of the card, where the crutches and canes hung in real life, were written the words, *"A la Grotte Bénie j'ai prié pour vous."* I didn't speak French so for all I knew, the words could have translated as, "After the Grotto, Benny will pour you a drink." I stifled a laugh. A forty-something woman sitting across from me looked up from her book, acknowledging my laugh and nodding my way.

"'Ello," she warmly offered in a light French accent.

"Hello! Do you speak English? Could you please tell me what is written on the card?" I held up the card as if I was a contestant on a quiz show revealing a final answer.

"I said a prayer for you at the grotto," she replied.

"Thank you," I said as she returned to her book and I to my card. How perfect. The sentiment fit. Knowing my mother's appreciation for a chilled martini, I was confident she would have liked both translations—the prayer *and* the drink at Benny's.

As the train jostled us to and fro, I sloppily wrote:

Dear Mom,

Mission accomplished…. I'm so glad I came here…. The town itself is very beautiful and surrounded by mountains. My own little story of coming to Lourdes is pretty funny—details will wait 'til later, but I traveled here with a guy named Adrian from Tasmania. Right now, I'm heading to Narbonne to spend the night. Tomorrow morning, I'll catch the train to Barcelona.

Love always,
Carla

I was no Emerson, Thoreau, or Strode, but I knew Mom would love it.

Blessing My Mother's Rosary

As the train continued to rock to the rhythm of track meeting terrain, I sat back and relaxed. The Occitan countryside whizzed by like a scene from a rear screen projector. While exciting to think I would soon set foot in Spain, it was difficult to leave Lourdes, which now held a place forever in my heart. And it got me to thinking: *Miracles abound. They are there for us to witness, experience, appreciate, and learn from—sometimes just by being more present and aware. The birth of a baby. Sunsets and moonrises. Flowers and trees born out of the embers of a devastating fire. The human generosity that arises after a natural or manmade disaster. A mother's love. Or simply the gift of another day on this precious planet we call Earth. Life itself is a miracle. The miracle is that it is ours to experience and celebrate anytime we want.*

I sat there, grateful for my miraculous life. Would I see Adrian again? Would I return to Lourdes? Only time would tell. I pulled out my bottle of water, taking a sip of the grotto's refreshing elixir. While I had sampled Lourdes and its water, I would never have my fill.

The Gift

—«««•»»»—

As the train took me further away from the City of Miracles, I remembered a song I had heard as a child. It was written by Eula Parker for a Christmas album my family routinely played. The song, "The Village of St. Bernadette," and its lyrics never meant more to me than they did in that moment:

> I've traveled far, the land and the sea,
> Beautiful places I happened to be,
> One little town I'll never forget,
> Is Lourdes, the village of Saint Bernadette.

—«««•»»»—

That song still loops around in my head even now, as I finish this little story. My Lourdes miracle is a pocket full of memories and a blessed rosary that secures in me the knowledge that I, too, have been blessed with a gift. A gift who is, was, and always will be…my mother.

QUESTION

What everyday miracles are *you* grateful for? Make a list.

EPILOGUE

Goodness Abounds
Goodness
is the only investment
that never fails.

Henry David Thoreau
Walden; or, Life in the Woods

112

I returned to Lourdes two years after my mother's death and thirty-seven years after my first visit there. I was sixty years old. The early morning mist heightened the sweet smells of the palm trees, orange-red poppies, purple and pink impatiens, bridal wreath spirea, and sprays of fountain grass. Clouds descended on the mountains in the distance and over the town's imposing fort with its French tricolor flapping in the breeze. It looked like a theatrical backdrop, dramatic and moody, but one-hundred-percent real.

I headed to the sanctuary. The morning mist had turned to a steady rain and this, coupled with an unrelenting wind, made it difficult to even walk. I joined many of the pilgrims dotting the esplanade as they tried righting their inverted umbrellas and played tug-of-war with the gusting foe.

Masses soon would begin in various locations, which presented the perfect opportunity for me to find a priest to "officially" bless my mother's rosary. Even though I knew in my heart that the rosary had been blessed on my first trip to Lourdes with Adrian, I had decided to return to make it "official." For me, it was unfinished business—a promise left to fulfill.

Blessing My Mother's Rosary

I made my way to the stairs leading to the entrance of the Basilica of Our Lady. I was joined by an Italian family, and together we began to ascend the steep staircase. As the granddaughter of Italian immigrants and the daughter of a mother who fluently spoke Italian, I felt she would be pleased that I had returned to Lourdes and now was making the final steps of the journey with fellow Italians.

The ramp and stairs were not an easy climb, which became more taxing with each step we took. It appeared the family matriarch was struggling as she let out a guttural prayer, "Oh, Madonne!" (Oh, Madonna!) It was a plea my mother routinely said for various reasons. Traffic jam? "Oh, Madonne!" Burnt pancakes? "Oh, Madonne!" Waking up to a foot of snow? "Oh, Madonne!" Misplaced keys or wallet? "Oh, Madonne!"

We continued our climb, with the matriarch rhythmically "Madonning" with each step she took. Mercifully, with one last step to go, she blurted out "Oh," made a pregnant pause, and then let out a final, "…Madonne!" as we arrived at the basilica's landing just in time for the midday service in Italian.

Walking through the massive doors, I discovered the basilica overflowing with thousands of Italians. Not only were the pews packed, but so too were the marble steps leading from the main floor to the side naves. The *stagiaires* in charge of the altar and vestments scurried about tending to their duties, readying the altar for the service. Attempting to locate the entrance to the sacristy, I followed their every move. It seemed they entered and exited from the right or, as it is often called, the "St. Joseph" side. I weaved my way through the crowd.

Reaching the far end of the side nave closest to the altar, I curled around the corner, stood in the sacristy doorway, and peered inside. With great anticipation, I pulled out my mother's rosary and held it in the palm of my cupped hand. There stood three priests dressed in white chasubles with colorful stoles draped around their shoulders. The priests were in deep conversation and, although I felt as if I were intruding, I was determined to complete my mission even if it meant standing there for hours.

It wasn't just the fact that getting her rosary blessed at Lourdes had been *one* of my mother's fervent wishes, but that it was the *last* of her requests to me. It was the only request of consequence she had made of me as a young woman that I felt had been somewhat unfulfilled.

I say "somewhat" because I knew in many ways that the rosary had been blessed by Adrian and me on my first trip to Lourdes and my mother was more than pleased with that. And even as I selfishly reasoned that still having a request of hers left to attend to was somehow keeping her alive in my heart, I also knew it was time to get it done "right." Her death and my finding the now-imperfect rosary pinned together with love only heightened my determination. I felt I was on the cusp of finally making good on my original promise and our common goal.

The eldest priest of the group suddenly looked in my direction, and with a countenance of compassion and gentility began walking towards me. I met him halfway.

"Good morning, Father," I said, "I'm sorry if I've interrupted you." The other two priests were watching the exchange intently. "I have travelled all the way from Chicago to get my mother's rosary blessed."

The priest extended an outstretched hand and I carefully placed the rosary in his palm, hoping he didn't see the safety pin holding it together. I feared he might invoke some obscure church rule—there's always a rule—that priests were forbidden to bless religious objects that were falling apart or not fully intact!

Instead, looking directly into my eyes which moistened with emotion, the priest, revealing a beautiful Italian accent, asked, "What is your name?" Although Mass was about to begin, he was calm and methodical, as though time was of no consequence.

"Carla," I replied, adding, "My mother, Mary, asked me to get this blessed when I was here in 1982, but it was late November and I couldn't find a priest. She recently passed away."

"Your mother has passed and you've brought her rosary here to be blessed?" he asked, making sure he had heard the details correctly. I nodded, looking into his soft, empathetic eyes. He began, "I bless this rosary in the name of the Father, the Son, and the Holy Spirit. Amen," making the sign of the cross over it as I simultaneously crossed myself. He gently placed it back into my hand, covering it with both of his.

"Thank you, Father. What is your name?"

"Father Rafael," he said with a smile and tilt of his head.

"Thank you. My mother would have been so happy and grateful." I didn't want to tell him, but I knew, that my mother would view the fact that Father Rafael was Italian as "the pistachio at the end of a cannoli"—an added delight.

Fr. Rafael nodded and half-bowed at the waist. I bowed back awkwardly, then turned and hurried away. I wanted to tell the entire congregation, their eyes following me as I waded through them towards the door, the significance of what happened. Most of all, I wanted to tell my mother.

I felt at that moment: *If only I could place the rosary she had made "real" into her warm and welcoming hands. If only I could see her eyes fill with tears—because they most certainly would—upon hearing the latest news about her favorite rosary.* If only I had tried harder to live my life without "if onlys" as she had wanted me to do. But sometimes there was no avoiding them.

I exited the Basilica. The rain continued to fall, but it could not dampen my spirits. I descended as if on a cloud down what I will forever call the "Oh, Madonne" staircase and headed to the Bernadette Chapel to do one last thing for my mother: light a candle.

Over six decades I had lit countless candles in churches, first with my mother and then for her. For we both believed that even as a candle burns away or flames out, it remains lit eternally in the heart. I approached the votive stand and selected the candle best suited for her. It reminded me of the small, simple votive she had lit daily at home. Lighting it, I sent heavenward a four-word silent prayer: *"Mom, we did it."*

I felt a range of emotions. Profound joy that our shared goal was finally accomplished. Profound sadness that we had crossed this particular finish line. Our quest was complete and with it, I felt, the last and only unfulfilled request of my mother. Holding on to her rosary as if for dear life, I was both buoyed and bereft. *Now what do I do?* I thought. But quickly, as if to soothe me as they had always done, my mother's words came back to me:

"Do good things."

"Live your life."

"Do your best."

"Be your own unique self."

While these were words of encouragement, they were also requests I knew she hoped I would fulfill throughout my life. While there was a finality to the rosary now having been twice-blessed, there was still so much work left to be done in service to her. The candle and my mother would continue to light my way.

Blessing My Mother's Rosary

Finally, as odd and even absurd as it seems, I realized that grief, like my mother, is a precious gift that propels me to honor her in all I do. Her death was not the end of our relationship; rather, it was the beginning of a richer, more complete one. It drives me to explore and seek to better understand her legacy and continued revelation in me. Her death has led me to an even deeper, spiritual relationship with her. If I quiet myself, listen closely, and remember our conversations and experiences together, I find answers to all my questions. She continues to lead me in all I do and transforms my life daily through her words, her love, her example, and her rosary, which I keep at my bedside.

It reminds me that my mother will always be with me and that goodness abounds, whether we see it or whether we don't. That unshakable belief has been my personal miracle of Lourdes.

Carla Knorowski
Chicago, Illinois
December 8, 2024

ABOUT THE AUTHOR

Author in 1982 at a market
in Europe (age twenty-three)

Author in 2023 at Notre-Dame Cathedral
in Paris (age sixty-three)

Carla Knorowski is the former CEO of the Abraham Lincoln Presidential Library Foundation and former President of the Naval War College Foundation. She currently serves as President and CEO of Thirteen-Fifty Philanthropy.

A member of the Society of Midland Authors and the Catholic Writers Guild, she co-authored, with James M. Cornelius, *Under Lincoln's Hat: 100 Objects that Tell the Story of His Life and Legacy* (Lyons Press, 2016); edited and contributed to the top-selling *Gettysburg Replies: The World Responds to Abraham Lincoln's Gettysburg Address* (Lyons Press, 2015); and also contributed to *Lincoln an Intimate Portrait* (*LIFE*, 2014).

In 1989, she volunteered at Lourdes as an official sanctuary *stagiaire* or intern, administering to the infirm in a variety of ways. She was awarded the National Order of Merit at the rank of Officer by the French Republic and serves on the board of directors of the Friends of Notre-Dame de Paris, the official U.S.-based charity rebuilding Notre-Dame Cathedral in Paris. She recently worked with the *Paris-Chicago*

About The Author

Comité to erect a bust of Abraham Lincoln in Paris' 8th *Arrondissement,* which was unveiled in May 2024. Carla has traveled to more than twenty-five cities or towns in the world named "Paris."

A lifelong resident of Chicago, Carla is a three-time graduate of the University of Illinois at Chicago.

ALSO AVAILABLE

The Rosary: Prayer by Prayer
and
Grieving *with Mary*
by Mary K. Doyle

*How We Can Suffer Our Sorrow
…and Become Wiser, Better, Gentler People*
by Pamela Smith, SS.C.M.

*The Chapel of the Immaculate Conception
Meditations on Mary by Seminarians at Mundelein Seminary*
compiled by Fr. David H. Mowry

*Where God Is at Home
Poems of God's Word and World
Illuminated by The Message*
by Irene Zimmerman, OSF

*The Death of a Parent
Reflections for Adults Mourning the
Loss of a Father or Mother*
by Delle Chapman

*Gentle Comforts
For Women Grieving the Loss of
Their Beloved Life Companion*
by Kathleen Paris

**www.actapublications.com
800-397-2282**

ADVANCE PRAISE
from Mothers, Daughters, Sisters

As I read Carla Knorowski's spiritual masterpiece, I felt as though I had met not only a companion on the journey but a spiritual friend. The story of her visit to Lourdes at age twenty-two, which would not be her last, is memorable and moving in its simplicity. Moving as well is her account of a chance encounter with a fellow young pilgrim, Adrian of Tasmania, which reveals how a "perfect" stranger can become the soulmate of a moment in time and the agent of a life-changing experience. The author's narrative is a living legacy to the memory of her mother and a testament to how the intertwined lives of one mother and daughter—despite their obvious differences in occupation, temperament, and life circumstances—can craft the missing links of a blessed rosary and become an act of genuine devotion in the process. — Pamela Smith, SS.C.M., author, *How We Can Suffer Out Sorrow… and Become Wiser, Better, Gentler People*

Only a few chapters into Carla Knorowski's intriguing parable, I was hooked. Her personal story parallels many of my own experiences with my parents, the Blessed Mother of Jesus, and spiritual pilgrimages. This book will feed your soul with hope, love, and encouragement—a necessary recipe for peace during your most challenging of days. — Mary K. Doyle, author, *The Rosary Prayer by Prayer, Grieving with Mary,* and *Fatima at 100 / Fatima Today*

For every one of us who has ever lost a loved one and tried to make sense of the ensuing void and grief. This, however, is more than a book about coping with grief. The author allows us to vicariously travel along on a spiritual journey that is both healing and revelatory. She reminds all of us—Catholic or not — of the power of prayer and the reason why saints and the Blessed Mother continue to walk with us in our most difficult times. — Judith Valente, author of *The Art of Pausing: Meditations for the Overworked and Overwhelmed* and *The Italian Soul: How to Savor the Full Joys of Life*

ADVANCE PRAISE
from Mothers, Daughters, Sisters

A touching story brimming with love of a daughter for her mother framed by a treasured rosary that is brought to Lourdes. Carla Knorowski makes her uplifting quest an adventure spanning decades. The love always shines through. — Maureen Orth, journalist, special correspondent for *Vanity Fair* magazine, author, *National Geographic* cover story "How the Virgin Mary Became the World's Most Powerful Woman"

A profoundly moving journey into the depths of faith, grief, and devotion. With remarkable honesty, Carla Knorowski shares tender experiences of the love and loss of her mother, leading readers through moments of heartache and healing that feel universal and deeply personal. This book is a gift for anyone seeking comfort, connection, and a renewed sense of hope. — J. Kim Penberthy, clinical psychologist and the Chester F. Carlson Professor of Psychiatry & Neurobehavioral Sciences at the University of Virginia School of Medicine, author of *Living Mindfully across the Lifespan: An Intergenerational Guide,* written with her daughter, Morgan Penberthy

Carla Knorowski takes us on a poignant spiritual journey as she completes her mother's desire to have her rosary blessed at Lourdes. No matter your religious belief, you are inspired by the passion of this dutiful daughter. What a beautiful testament to the love between a parent and child. — Chaz Ebert, author, *It's Time to Give a FECK: Elevating Humanity through Forgiveness, Empathy, Compassion, and Kindness*

A story of love, faith, and memory. In other words, it's our story as much as it belongs to Carla Knorowski. Readers will be grateful that Carla set down this beautiful remembrance of her mother as gently and vividly as she did. And then they'll buy another copy for a special woman in their lives. I know I will. — Alice Camille, author, *The Rosary: Mysteries of Joy, Light, Sorrow, and Glory*